"I absolutely enjoyed reading *The Rooms in Your House*. Wendy Knipp draws you in with real-life stories and scenarios that will empower you to create boundaries for healthy friendships and relationships. What was also interesting and important to me was acknowledging that I could see myself in these scenarios as well. Recognizing these traits in myself inspires me to become a better friend to others—an important aspect of living life with fulfilling connections!"

—**Lisa King Rph**, The Fulfilled Pharmacist

"As someone who works in a high-pressure environment, I understand the importance of setting clear boundaries to maintain balance and focus. *The Rooms in Your House* offers practical and insightful strategies for establishing healthy personal boundaries, which are just as critical in our friendships as they are in our professional lives. This book is a valuable resource for anyone looking to foster stronger, more fulfilling relationships while protecting their own well-being."

—**Rick Nunley**, Managing Director, Investments

"*The Rooms in Your House* offers strategies to shift your mindset in order to build stronger relationships with friends, family, and colleagues. Combining relatable scenarios and practical advice with research-based insights, the author guides readers through delicate situations, emphasizing that real friendships thrive on mutual respect and understanding. This book dives into setting healthy boundaries without guilt, recognizing toxic patterns, and maintaining self-respect while being a supportive friend. The author emphasizes on why boundaries matter and how they can lead to more authentic and fulfilling relationships. Perfect for anyone who is looking to deepen their connections while preserving their own well-being!"

—**Gala Greenberg**, @gatherwithgala, Scottsdale, Arizona

THE
ROOMS
IN YOUR
HOUSE

A PRACTICAL GUIDE TO FRIENDSHIPS
AND PERSONAL BOUNDARIES

WENDY KNIPP

*b inspire*books

Published by Inspire Books
www.inspire-books.com

Cover and Interior Design by Inspire Books

Hardback ISBN: 979-8-9914784-2-7
Paperback ISBN: 979-8-9914784-0-3
e-book ISBN: 979-8-9914784-1-0
Library of Congress Control Number: 2024918484

Contents

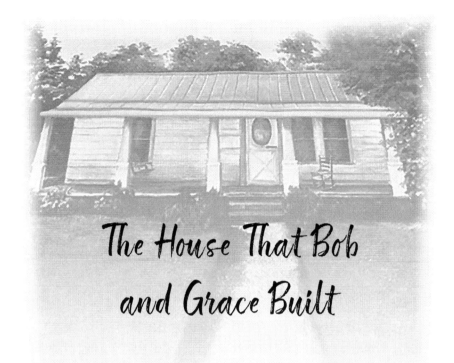

The House That Bob and Grace Built

We all have a foundation—a place that feels like a true safe haven, where boundaries are respected and unconditional support surrounds us. For me, that place was my grandparents' house, which they built themselves and which I've included in this book through a cherished photo. The cover of this book is inspired by their home—a tribute to the first place where I felt safe, loved, and completely at ease.

I can't say for certain when Bob and Grace first laid eyes on each other, but I can tell you that their love was unmistakable, a kind of love that transcended time and generations, touching not only their seven children but rippling out to me and my family. Their love built more than a family—it built a home, one that stood as a symbol of the values and lessons I carry with me to this day.

The story begins in the winter of 1909. Bob, born into a large family on the farmlands of middle Tennessee, grew up knowing that life was simple but demanding. From a young age, he learned that hard work wasn't just a choice—it was the very fabric of survival. But what carried him through the hardest days wasn't just grit or perseverance; it was his unwavering faith in the Lord. I'm told that when he passed, in the middle of a church service no less, his last words were, "Father, I come to thee." That was Bob—always ready, steadfast in his beliefs and unshaken by life's challenges.

In the summer of 1912, Grace was born, also into a large family. Though their paths wouldn't cross until years later, Grace, too, was shaped by a strong foundation of love and faith. When they finally met, the connection was undeniable. By 1929, they were married, and together they began building the life—and the family—they had dreamed of.

Bob worked long hours in the coal mines, his hands and lungs bearing the weight of the work. The darkness of the mines was a stark contrast to the bright love he shared with Grace.

In 1931, their first child—my father—was born, the first of seven. Life wasn't easy, but they found joy in each other, in their growing family, and in their shared faith. By 1938, they had saved enough money to buy two acres of land for thirty-five hard-earned dollars. It was there, on that humble plot of land, that Bob and Grace would build the home that graces the opening of this chapter.

The house began as just two rooms: a kitchen with a coal stove and a single room where the entire family—two adults and four children at the time—slept together. It was cramped, to say the least, but love filled the space between those walls. They didn't have much, but what they did have was shared freely, with the belief that family was their greatest treasure.

It was in this room each night that Bob would kneel down and pray, his quiet faith filling the space with a sense of peace and reverence. His children remember this ritual fondly—the image of their father in deep prayer, completely undistracted and unwavering in his devotion.

As the years went on, Bob's time in the coal mines took a toll on his health, and in 1942, he set out to find a new way to provide for his family. Day after day, he would walk for miles, sometimes over an hour, in search of work. Eventually, he found a job at Sewanee Military Academy, known today as the University of the South. The academy would transport workers during the week, but on weekends, Bob often walked the long journey home on his own. He would save what little food he had to ensure his children were fed, and though times were tough, the men he worked with often shared their meals with him. It was a quiet kindness, but it meant everything to Bob and Grace.

By 1947, the porch had been enclosed to create a proper kitchen, and for the first time, they added an indoor bathroom. Piece by piece, they continued to build that home—not just with wood and nails but with love and faith. The house remained humble, at 932 square feet for nine people, but it was never just about the size of the rooms. What truly mattered was what those rooms represented: forgiveness, respect, boundaries, and a love that never wavered, no matter how tough life became. It was in that kitchen that birthdays were celebrated with a child's favorite meal and always a cake.

Sixteen years before I was born, in the early 1950s, Bob and Grace added a porch swing to the front of the house. That swing became more than just a place to rest; it became a sacred space, where family and friends gathered to share stories, laughter, and sometimes tears. It was also where I learned, long before I understood the concept of boundaries, that relationships and friendships should make you feel good, they should make you feel safe.

Some of my clearest childhood memories are from that swing, sitting next to my redheaded grandmother, sipping Coke from a glass bottle, feeling the steady rhythm of the swing, and basking in the warmth of her presence. In those moments, surrounded by my family, I couldn't have articulated what boundaries were, but I could feel the love and respect that flowed through every interaction. It was as if they all knew how to give each other space, how to listen when needed, and how to come together when it mattered. It felt right.

Even though I didn't fully understand it at the time, I can look back now and realize that those moments on the porch were the foundation of my understanding of boundaries. My father's family showed me that relationships—whether with family, friends, or even yourself—should be built on respect, kindness, and love. They didn't need to teach me with words; the lessons were there in the way they treated each other, in the way they made everyone feel welcome yet honored personal space. I felt it, even as a child.

But it wasn't until I grew older that I truly understood what those feelings meant. As life unfolded, I came to realize that boundaries weren't just about creating distance; they were about fostering closeness in a healthy, respectful way. They were about protecting the things that mattered most: love, trust, and respect. The feeling I had on that porch—the safety, the comfort, the warmth—that's what I came to recognize as the foundations of a good relationship. That's what I now seek in friendships and connections: a place where I can be myself, where I can give and receive love without fear of overstepping or being overwhelmed.

Looking back, that little house was more than just a building. My Tennessee family taught me that boundaries weren't limitations—they were the framework for love. And though it took me years to fully understand, I now know that the love I felt on that porch swing was made possible because of those invisible lines of respect, patience, and care. In that small house, built by two people who worked so hard for everything they had, I learned the most important lesson of all: that love flourishes where boundaries are honored.

Now, as I raise my own family, I carry those lessons with me. The house may have been small, but its legacy is strong. It wasn't just four walls—it was a foundation for life, built on faith, love, and the quiet strength of boundaries.

Foreword

I find it somewhat ironic that I am writing the foreword for a book about rooms in a house when I was seventeen years old before I lived in a house that didn't have wheels under it or multi-purpose rooms. Let me explain. My father was in pipeline construction in the 1950s and 1960s, which necessitated that the seven members of our household share a two-bedroom, one-bath trailer—a house on wheels that enabled us to travel together as a family. Needless to say, we grew up close!

We followed that work all over the US moving no fewer than eighty-nine times before I finished my freshman year of high school. That meant changing schools a lot—thirty-one times to be exact. I actually attended six different schools one year!

This becomes relevant when you translate those moves into relationships. Growing up, I would imagine you likely had friendships with several dozen classmates. My number would have easily exceeded a thousand. Being the 'new kid on the block' and wanting to 'fit in' meant I had to make friends quickly. In doing so, I became an open book, welcoming everyone into my world who showed the least bit of interest.

When I would invite my new friends over to visit, it's important to understand there were no curbs in the trailer park that separated our house from the street. Nor were there porches to sit on. They would come directly into our living room and kitchen since the two were combined because of the limited space. Little did I know this would carry over into my adult life—not physically, but emotionally.

The significance of this came to light when I began reading this manuscript by Wendy Knipp. In The Rooms in Your House, I discovered the importance of having a Curb, a Porch, a Living Room, and a Kitchen for those relationships. Each room represented a different level of connection, of comfort, of trust, of intimacy. Wendy's vision would provide a simple yet powerful visual to help me see which "room" the people in my life truly belonged.

Within the first few pages of her book, I had an epiphany. I realized that when I became an adult, I continued to repeat the ill-fated behaviors of my youth. I was letting far too many people into my Living Room and Kitchen and much too early—individuals who I now know should have been on the Curb or the Porch. I was too trusting, too forgiving, too vulnerable, too anxious to make that new friend. And it cost me—and unfortunately others—in more ways than I care to divulge. Life lesson learned.

After completing the manuscript, it became obvious that I needed to reassess many of the relationships in my life. And not just for me—for the benefit of everyone in my "house." I'm in the early stages of this, but I already see the payoff. My Living Room and Kitchen are no longer overcrowded. I'm creating more time for the few who deserve to be in those rooms. As a result, those relationships are becoming deeper, more meaningful, more fulfilling. I treasure them more than ever. I can thank Wendy for that.

As you read this piece of brilliance—I don't say that lightly . . . it is nothing short of brilliant—my hope is that you, too, will have an epiphany. That you will gain an awareness of the importance of taking control of your life. It's becoming a game-changer for me. I trust it will be for you.

Now it's time for you to do some spring cleaning. Turn the page and prepare to improve the quality of your relationships . . . and your life!

Steve Rigby

Consultant, Trainer, Speaker

Author of Amazon Best Seller *S.M.I.L.E.*

Foreword

I t's been a privilege to know Wendy for over a decade, both as a friend and a business collaborator. Over these years, I've had the joy of witnessing her incredible journey, both professionally and personally. *The Rooms in Your House* is a book that truly captures the essence of Wendy's passion for genuine connection and her talent for navigating the beautiful—and sometimes complex—dance of friendship and personal boundaries.

Beyond our work together, I have followed Wendy's journey through her online presence, particularly her website, Socially Brave, and her Instagram page. Through her stories and advice, one thing stood out above all: Wendy's commitment to becoming her truest self. Her dedication to personal growth and authenticity was a natural magnet, and it's something I wanted to share with others. This led me to invite her as the keynote speaker for a women's panel I was hosting at an industry event. Though she was a bit hesitant at first, taking the time to consider and pray over the decision, she ultimately agreed. And I couldn't have been more thrilled—because, truthfully, I wasn't taking "no" for an answer anyway!

When Wendy took the stage, she brought the room to life, leading the audience through moments of laughter, reflection, and even a few tears. The buzz of her speech carried on for days, and I felt an immense sense of pride in watching her step into that role with such grace and power.

For those new to Wendy's work, you're in for something truly special. As you read on, you'll discover that, in Wendy's world, friendship isn't just a word; it's a room where boundaries, trust, and warmth come together to form connections that truly matter. And if you're wondering what it means to have a friend in your "kitchen"—a place reserved for those closest to you—you'll soon understand why Wendy's there for me.

The Rooms in Your House isn't just a book; it's an invitation to examine your own relationships and find where you—and your people—fit best.

Sharon Bartlett
Executive Director of Operations
US REO Partners

Introduction

Are you currently struggling, or have you struggled in the past with friendships, whether with acquaintances, co-workers, long-term friends, or even certain friendships with family members? Maybe you've experienced a betrayal of trust, a painful friendship breakup, or the frustration of someone who consistently drains your emotional energy.

When you are in an emotional state because one person after another is betraying or belittling you, it deeply hurts your heart. If you have ever experienced this, I don't need to tell you about the pain. While you are curled up in an emotional ball of hurt, you wonder *why* the people who betrayed you can go about their day, oblivious to your suffering.

To them, you are behaving like a wounded animal. While you replay the hurt over and over, they barely remember the words or actions that created the hurt inside. Each time you meet, they behave in a way that suggests you are the problem, so you open up again, and the cycle continues.

You've probably heard of boundaries at one point or another in life, and you may even have tried to set some with friends and family. But to truly appreciate the power of healthy boundaries in your life, it's helpful to have a framework to visualize where people stand with you. Is there someone you want to be friends with? What type of a friend would be good for you? One who fills your heart and makes you feel good when you are around them, one who doesn't make you feel like you have to play games or walk on eggshells, worrying if you said something wrong. I bet you have never asked that question before . . . I know I never did. The standard boundaries idea uses circles—for example, an inner circle of friends and an outer circle. For me, I was unable to conceptualize this idea; it was too broad of a range, but the unique concept I propose in this book truly revolutionized the way I understood relationships and freed me from so much conflict, guilt, and heartbreak.

It's all about the Rooms in Your House.

With so many people in and out of your life, sometimes on a daily basis, where should they all go? Imagine a house with different rooms representing the varying levels of trust you share with people. The Curb is where you will first meet and where some acquaintances will stay—those you greet with a smile but don't let into your personal space. The Porch is for friends you enjoy but may not fully share your personal stories with. The Living Room is reserved for those you trust deeply, where vulnerability is met with understanding and respect. And the Kitchen? Now, that's sacred ground, where the closest relationships have developed with love, support, and authenticity.

I designed this concept because I needed a way to visualize people and their behaviors in a way that resonated with me. Saying someone was in my "inner circle" never quite captured the different relationships in my life. Each time I saw certain individuals, I found myself being vulnerable with them, even when I shouldn't have been. We had not yet formed an authentic connection built on trust. This framework allows me to recognize where they belong in my home—whether they're on the Curb or enjoying time on the Porch—I can approach each interaction with awareness and intention.

By understanding the Rooms in Your House, you can navigate your relationships with greater confidence, knowing who deserves a place in your home of trust and who might need to stay outside. Let's explore this journey together and discover how building these figurative rooms can lead to richer, more fulfilling friendships—ones that will make you feel good when you are around them.

In this concept, the Curb is the initial place for new relationships. When you first meet someone, this is where they should start. It's also where some relationships may remain permanently. The Curb acts as a transition zone, allowing time for the relationship to take its natural course. The Porch is for friends we are getting to know; we keep the information we share on a social level, and we have fun and enjoy their company. More than likely, this will be our largest group of friends. Living Room friends have earned our trust through experiences; we have shared personal information, and they have not betrayed our trust. Kitchen friends are the closest anyone can get to us; here in the Kitchen, we are open and vulnerable. It has been my experience that this is where few people in my circle of friends are.

People have to cultivate trust with you in order to change rooms. You can establish which room they belong in by noticing their behavior and their ability to keep secrets, build trust, and honor your boundaries. This is not to say they have to earn their way to be a friend or need to do things monetarily, but their room placement is based on how you want to be treated and the respect you offer each other in relationships.

The Rooms in Your House concept offers a visual representation of friendship boundaries, which can help us better understand and communicate our needs within our social circles. By categorizing relationships into different "rooms," we can gain insight into the varying levels of trust and intimacy present in each relationship, leading to more conscious and informed decisions about the level of disclosure and emotional investment in each friendship. It also helps us see red flags (or green or yellow ones) sooner and more clearly.

> "We learn what to expect from people based on what they show us over time. Safe people are those who draw us closer to who we were meant to be spiritually, emotionally, and mentally. They are individuals who consistently reflect traits of respect, honesty, and compassion."[1]

The term "red flag" typically refers to a character trait or behavior that is a warning signal or sign of deeper issues. Generally, we are able to feel when something is off before we can articulate the pattern of behavior. There are standard red flag signals that we adhere to, and we have our own signals based on relationships of the past. With friendships, a red flag is a sign that a person's behavior might be unhealthy, signaling to you to proceed with caution or distance yourself. A green flag means the friendship is healthy and supportive, with trust and mutual respect. A yellow flag suggests there might be some concerns and potential issues, so it's wise to pay attention and see how things

---

[1] Dr. Henry Cloud and Dr. John Townsend, *Safe People: How to Find Relationships that are Good for You and Avoid Those That Aren't* (Tennessee: Zondervan, 2016).

develop before fully committing or, in our case, moving someone into a new room space.

We need to understand and recognize the characteristics of safe people: those with whom we don't have to second-guess or question whether we can trust they won't betray our trust. This will allow us to understand their reliability and trustworthiness, regardless of their actions in the moment. We will review the "rooms" concept to understand how it helps in establishing boundaries and recognizing different levels of friendships while fostering healthy boundaries with a wide range of individuals.

Everyone Needs Boundaries!

You have picked up this book, so on some level, I'm guessing you know you're missing something in your relationships, but you're not sure what it is. Maybe this is the first time in a long time you have the courage to stand up and say, "I'm choosing me," or you are not 100 percent sure you understand how boundaries work. I want to let you know you have come to the right place! I have been where you are right now and know this is a journey worth taking. We will learn how healthy relationship boundaries are crucial for emotional well-being and maintaining fulfilling connections with others.

Throughout this book, I have created fictional scenarios based on events early on in my life, as well as situations I helped navigate others through, to illustrate the dynamics of each room in your house, and I've changed the names and situational details to protect privacy. I've had a lifetime of experience walking through challenging relationships and years devoted to therapy, research, and my own personal development. I also have over ten years of experience in life coaching and the personal development of others, and I've dedicated my career to empowering people to create healthier relationships with themselves and others. It is my passion to encourage and equip others to walk in their purpose, and I'm so glad you've decided to join me in learning the Rooms in Your House.

Not everyone in your life will need to be placed in a room space in your house. It can be an eye-opening experience but well worth it as you establish this as another step in your journey of self-care and realization.

My goal is not to call anyone out or to put shame on others; we are all on our own journey, and I know I had my share of times when my boundaries were not in check. I can honestly say I have worked hard to understand the shame associated with a lack of boundaries, and others don't need to understand or agree with the way I create my boundaries. We don't know what we don't know, and growth happens at a different pace for everyone.

This will be a journey of understanding behaviors in ourselves and others. It will not be without challenges! Establishing boundaries can lead to difficulties in asserting your needs, feeling overwhelmed by the demands of others, and experiencing pushback in creating a sense of personal strength.

I'm proud of you for taking this step. More importantly, you should be proud of yourself. With a clear understanding, support, and time, it is possible for you to harness the power of boundaries to develop healthier relationship dynamics. I'm excited for you—this will be a worthwhile journey that will lead to self-empowerment, greater understanding, and more peace in your heart and relationships.

Let's do this!

CHAPTER 1

The Rooms in Your House

Laura was someone I had known for years. She embodied everything I aspired to be—poised, stylish, and effortlessly in control. Growing up in a lower-middle-class family, I often felt out of place, longing to be anyone but myself. Laura was the kind of friend who seemed to have it all together—kind, calm, and always composed.

As our friendship deepened, I felt comfortable confiding in her, believing she was a safe space for my thoughts and feelings. Yet, I soon learned that the stories I shared with her were often relayed to others, leaving me feeling exposed and vulnerable. Looking back, I recognize the red flags I overlooked, signs of betrayal that I was too naïve to see at the time. Without boundaries, I had no understanding of what to look for.

The manipulation ran so deep that I don't think she realized it was happening. I later discovered that Laura, too, had her own struggles rooted in generational dysfunction. Whenever we were together, I felt small. She would criticize my voice, my clothing choices, and how I interacted with her friends. "They don't really like you," she would say, "but if you just fit in more, they'll come around." I was lost in a cycle of self-doubt, believing her words were meant to help me when, in reality, they were tearing me down.

Time and again, I confided in her, convinced that she had my best interests at heart. Each betrayal cut deeper than the last, leaving me heartbroken and confused. I remember pacing in my bathroom, venting to my husband about the latest hurt: "She did it again!" Each revelation felt like a fresh wound, and I was left wondering why I couldn't find a friend who would love me unconditionally.

My husband was giving me all the advice he could: "Why do you let her get to you like that? You are giving her too much power over you." Honestly, I couldn't see how what he was saying could help me. It never stopped me from trying to connect. I was drowning in shame, a dichotomy of wanting to share and connect to needing to disconnect from her and share nothing. Just when the pain and crying stopped from the last time, I was betrayed again. My words were being used against me with other people, and I was being represented as the person causing the issues.

> It was devastating. Crying was daily at this point; my relationship with others suffered, yet I was told I was overreacting. I was on this emotional roller coaster, and it was killing me inside.

t's been over thirty years, and I can still recall that moment with vivid details—the raw emotions, where I was standing, who I was talking to, and how I paced back and forth crying, wondering, again, what I did wrong and why they were doing this to me. I wanted so badly to have close friends in my life, that one group of people that I could confide in, share my dreams with, and encourage each other. I wanted to belong and for others to see me as I am.

First and foremost, I want you to understand that setting boundaries is an act of self-respect and is fundamental to any healthy relationship. Being explicit about your boundaries and upholding them is vital. If you're new to the idea of boundaries, here's a simple definition:

> Boundaries in friendships are like the walls and doors of a house, providing structure and safety. They help us communicate our needs, values, and limits to others, ensuring that our relationships are built on mutual respect and understanding.

Healthy boundaries allow us to express what we are comfortable with—whether it's how much time we spend together, the types of conversations we engage in, or how we support one another during tough times. They empower us to say "no" when we need to, without feeling guilty. Friendship boundaries also help us identify the level of trust we can give to different friends. Just as we wouldn't invite everyone into our living room, we shouldn't feel obligated to share our innermost thoughts and feelings with everyone we meet. Not everyone deserves to be in your kitchen. Understanding where each person fits within the "rooms" allows us to cultivate deeper connections with those who truly respect and honor our boundaries.

Ultimately, boundaries are about creating healthy relationships that enrich our lives rather than drain us. As you navigate the process of sharing yourself with others in various relationships, you will need to establish boundaries and remain mindful of them, adapting them as needed to ensure that the relationship stays mutually respectful and enriching.

The initial phase of a friendship lays the groundwork for trust. Respecting boundaries is crucial during this time, as overstepping them can indicate a lack of respect or understanding, which, in turn, can erode the trust necessary for a deeper connection.

The concept of the rooms is designed to safeguard our emotional well-being. If someone disregards our boundaries prematurely, it can leave us feeling exposed or threatened, which is counterproductive to fostering a secure relationship. Comfort with personal boundaries varies from individual to individual. When boundaries are crossed without regard, it can lead to discomfort, potentially causing tension in a new friendship.

The way boundaries are handled at the start often establishes the tone for the entire relationship. Allowing others to overstep your boundaries without addressing your friend can create a recurring pattern of disrespect. You will get to the point where you don't trust your own judgment.

Maintaining boundaries is not about keeping others at arm's length but about nurturing a healthy, respectful, and mutually gratifying relationship. When boundaries are honored, both people can feel secure enough to progressively reveal more of themselves, enabling the friendship to develop at a pace that is comfortable for all parties involved.

Growing up, I was painfully unaware of boundaries—what they were, how to create them, or that I even needed them. Relationships to me were hard to figure out, and building them was somewhat of a mystery to me. I was that one person who thought everyone was on the same boundary level all the time. You were either a close friend or not a part of my life at all. If I had known you for a long period of time, you were, in my mind, someone who I could confide in and share details of my life regardless of how you treated me or whether you shared my secrets.

Looking back now, I was so naive. I'm sure you are wondering, just as I did, how could I not know how to establish healthy friendships?

To be honest, I would need to go deep into my childhood for this purpose, and I will not. That, my friend, is another story for another time. Perhaps it's a book in the making—with a working title of *The Appliance Baby*. Right? It's catchy and an insight to why I may not have understood that boundaries can go back to generational dysfunction.

Unhealthy Boundaries from Childhood Dysfunction

I come from generational dysfunction; this is where some dysfunctions have been passed down from generation to generation, usually based on shame and lack of boundaries. I will say, as with most parents, mine did the best they could with the knowledge they had. And to be honest, I wouldn't be writing this book and helping others through the process without having the childhood experience I had. I wouldn't want anyone to go through what I did, but it has made me who I am today.

I am the youngest of six children to parents who themselves did not understand boundaries, hence generational dysfunction. The discipline method back then was based on fear, guilt, and shame. I had to evaluate the mood of the people in the house and adjust accordingly. Being latchkey kids, we had to fend for ourselves. It was all about survival in my home. Boundaries—what was that? We were just trying to get through the day.

Because of their parenting styles, I didn't know what boundaries were, I was in situations that I should not have been in, and I was always playing the victim role. I now know that as we begin to develop relationship boundaries in early childhood, we start to differentiate ourselves from others and understand personal space and autonomy.

Relationship boundaries continue throughout adolescence and into adulthood because we are influenced by experiences, cultural norms, and social interactions. Between generational differences and the struggles many face growing up themselves, the dysfunctional cycle continues until one person in a generation decides the cycle needs to be broken.

Life without Boundaries Is No Life at All

I was going through life with an open wound most of the time, feeling victimized over and over due to the lack of boundaries that should have navigated me toward healthy relationships and a peaceful life.

According to an article by VeryWellMind, a person's "sense of self (not just their surface-level behavior) may change depending on the situation and the people they're with at the moment."[2] As it did for me growing up, this behavior could stem from a deep-seated desire for acceptance and validation, leading to unconsciously adopting the characteristics, behaviors, and opinions of those around me in an attempt to fit in and gain approval. Another way to look at this is to say that I didn't have my own opinions or very little of my own values.

Having a sense of self is necessary when establishing friendships. In her book *The Gifts of Imperfections*, Brené Brown emphasizes the importance of self-awareness and a strong sense of self when setting boundaries in friendships: "Daring to set boundaries is about having the courage to love ourselves, even when we risk disappointing others."[3] Brené speaks to the idea that a healthy sense of self is fundamental to establish boundaries and that knowing and honoring our own needs, values, and limitations empowers us to create friendships where

---

[2] Sanjana Gupta, "Identity Diffusion: Unraveling the Mystery of Self-Concept," *VeryWellMind.com*, May 18, 2023, https://www.verywellmind.com/identity-diffusion-causes-effects-how-to-find-yourself-7499502.

[3] Brené Brown, *The Gifts of Imperfection: Let Go of Who You Think You're Supposed to Be and Embrace Who You Are* (Minnesota: Hazelden Publishing, 2022), 45.

respect and mutual understanding can grow. This self-respect lays the groundwork for boundaries that support genuine and balanced relationships.

I can recall early in my therapy when I would describe the times I felt the need to be fake with people in my life. It was bothersome to me I never felt that I was me; I always felt as if I had to be what they wanted instead of who I was.

Looking back, I realize I was mimicking, a type of people-pleasing to ensure I was liked by others. Having yet to develop a sense of self, I had no idea how to create boundaries, and I had no opinions or little beliefs of my own.

Without a clear understanding of your own identity and boundaries, you may struggle to assert individuality and may instead adapt to the expectations and preferences of others. The saying goes, *If you stand for nothing, you will stand for all things.* This pattern of behavior can hinder the development of authentic and healthy relationships, as well as contribute to a sense of internal conflict and dissatisfaction.

The Breaking Point

I wish I could say that the moment standing in the bathroom crying was my breaking point, where I had finally decided I was not going to live this way, and my mental health was worth fighting for. The reality is it was just the beginning of my journey. It would be a few more years before understanding the rooms in my house and that I was worthy of respect and peace in my heart.

I was in a period in my life where my personal journey was exhausting me. I was, in my core, losing myself, unable to make decisions on what I wanted out of life. Finding myself without any future dreams or goals and getting to the point where I could no longer trust my own judgment, this started me on my self-healing, self-care journey of learning healthy boundaries and loving myself. It wasn't one specific event that drove me to have better boundaries; it was, however, a specific feeling of being so out of touch with myself and watching the people around me living a happy existence, unaware of what they were doing to me—I was the only one suffering. That was when I had to decide this was no longer acceptable.

The situation with Laura from the chapter's opening story would not be the last situation I would need to overcome; however, it was the beginning of my understanding of boundaries and why being open in what was shared was unhealthy in establishing friendships.

It is clear now that I suffered from poor relationship boundaries; what I wasn't unaware of at the time was I didn't have boundaries at all. I didn't even know that I was supposed to have rules in relationships.

After years of therapy, reading books, research, and the practice of healthy boundary setting, the rawness of my wounds healed, and I was in a good place where creating boundaries with friends was not so overwhelming. My confidence in myself was building.

Discovering the Concept of Rooms in the House

In my journey of self-help and understanding human behavior, I heard an analogy of the windows in a house—how others see you, how you see yourself, etc. To be honest, it probably came from my therapist at the time, Cinthia, who helped me understand the world around me, to see things through others' eyes, and helped me realize I am loved just the way I am. That got me thinking about the rooms in a house and the people in my life.

One day, as I was thinking about the windows, I was deeply hurt by a real-life *Mean Girls* scenario. I was out with a friend who answered a call from another person in our friend group. Unfortunately, I could hear both sides of the conversation, and their words were not flattering to me. Shocked and hurt, I thought, "Forget the window—they should both be at the curb."

I understood in that moment that there were people who needed to be placed where they could not see into the windows of my life or have access to my inner sanctum. Over time, I refined the concepts based on behavior and realized Curb friends could sometimes move to my Porch where trust could be developed.

The Rooms in Your House has provided peace, joy, and self-confidence in my life. My hope in sharing it is that you, too, will have the courage to create boundaries for more joy and peace in your life as well.

Let's take a tour of the different Rooms in Your House and discover who inhabits each of them.

The Curb

The starting place for all new relationships. Here, you can observe and evaluate whether they will stay at the Curb or move to the Porch. This stage is crucial for determining the potential depth of the relationship without oversharing. This is where you need to be aware of the flags and slowly build trust. While it is not a room, it is where relationships start and where some will stay.

The Porch

The porch is a room or, in my case, a place where most of your friends will stay. This is the front porch for me; you can have a back porch or any room you feel serves as the place for individuals you socialize with or enjoy being around. These are friends with whom you have mutual interests, respect, and enjoy being their company. I personally have three levels on the Porch, and as I get to know each person and their values and we build trust, they will go to the next level, where I will share more of who I am and what my goals are. By keeping these relationships on the Porch, you can enjoy their company without compromising your emotional well-being. You can have fun with them, enjoy their company, and, heck, you can travel with them if you want! However, what you cannot share on the Porch is information you do not want anyone else to know.

The Living Room

This room is reserved for the people you know well and who have demonstrated they are safe and trustworthy. You have built trust based on situations in your life; they were there to support you and want the best for you. They have not shared your secrets, and you feel safe with them. They are supportive, and you can share intimate information, dreams, and hopes for the future with them. The people in the Living Room form your core support system.

The Kitchen

This is the most trusted room in the house, reserved for a very small circle of individuals you can count on—your "ride or die" friends. They've proven themselves over time and through various life experiences to be trustworthy and faithful.

Just like a house, our lives are filled with different individuals, each playing a unique role in our growth and well-being. By recognizing where each person belongs, we can create healthier boundaries that nurture relationships, allowing us to flourish with those who uplift, support, and empower us. This understanding helps us build a space of peace and positivity, where meaningful connections can thrive.

Over the next few chapters, you'll learn how to place people in the appropriate rooms of your house, allowing you to create boundaries that nurture healthier, more fulfilling relationships. Some relationships may evolve quickly, while others take time, but everyone deserves a designated space. Whether it's significant others, family members, coworkers, or casual acquaintances, being aware of where each person stands helps ensure every interaction contributes to your well-being and growth.

To facilitate this process, you can mentally note who belongs where or utilize the blank pages provided in each chapter to list people and the rooms they belong. As you progress through the book, you can add or remove names as needed. By the end, you will have a clear understanding of who occupies each room in your house.

To further clarify your reasoning, jot down a few notes next to each person's name. For example:

Curb - *Donna, family member, tends to share my private information with others, undermines my relationships with other family members, yet pretends we are very close.*

Curb - *Katherine, known for two months, haven't spent enough time with her to evaluate trust.*

Curb - *Maria, known since high school, she was once a trusted friend, and because I believed and trusted her, I didn't recognize the signs of betrayal. Because I graced her in several times, she now needs to be on the Porch, and because I don't have her out of my life, she will go to the Curb if she has not course-corrected her actions.*

Porch - *Maddy, friend I have known for a while; she is fun, and we have shared interests; however, Kathy is not in a place in life where she wants more from a friend; therefore, she stays on the Porch.*

Porch - *Rose, a friend I have known for a while; she is a friend of a friend, and I love hanging out with her; she is kind, loving, and always* positive. However, we have not spent enough time together to establish trust; therefore, she stays on my Porch.

Porch - Amber is a friend I have known since we were kids in grade school; however, over the years, she has become negative and has a drama-filled life. She will remain on the first level of the Porch.

Living Room - Mia and Emerald, known for three years, they have shared personal information with me, and I have shared with them. They have not shared what I have said with others. They don't share with others in our friend group. My vulnerability has been protected.

Kitchen - Wally, known since I was seventeen, has always had my best interests at heart, never betrayed my trust.

It's important to note these are not physical rooms in our homes; they are relational rooms to help us visually and emotionally protect our inner thoughts and help ensure we do not share too much of ourselves. In the following chapters, we'll go deeper into each room, who belongs there, and what happens when they need to be moved from one relational room to the next.

The Rooms in Your House are for *your* boundaries. They were designed to protect your boundaries. While we are all curious as to where we fit in others' rooms, it's about how others fit into our lives. Let's assume your lifelong friend, for you, is a Living Room friend. You trust her and feel comfortable with sharing personal information. What if your friend has a different idea of what a close relationship looks like, and to her, you are a Kitchen or a Porch friend? It does not change the value of the relationship. You see, where you are in the rooms of her house is not as important as where she is in the rooms of your house. The concept of the "rooms" and this book is about protecting your personal boundaries.

We have people in our lives that we want to be close with, and we want the ability to trust them even though they repeatedly do and say things that abuse our boundaries and refuse to acknowledge their part in the relationship. We will learn to evaluate when it's a good time to emotionally move them from one room to another and why.

Most of us have that one person in our life with whom we want to be in a close relationship; however, they use our words against us, we separate from them, and when we meet up again, they give us the illusion we can trust them, we are vulnerable, then we are betrayed, yet again.

Typically, when we don't have boundaries, the process plays out in this way: They do or say things that abuse our trust one day, and on a different day, they mimic our behavior, we feel we can trust them, and once again we are vulnerable only to be betrayed again. These are individuals who can be co-workers, friends, or family members.

By putting people in the proper relational rooms, you will able to keep the relationships in perspective, where they are in the house regardless of how they are behaving, and you will not be fooled by their ability to seem safe enough for you to share information and then be betrayed when they use your words against you. No longer will you be fooled by temporary actions; if they are on your Curb, for example, no matter what they say or how they treat you in the short term, they have not earned the right to know your dreams and goals.

This helps keep things on a safe level for good mental health; it will stop you from oversharing, and your inner thoughts will be safe. You can still keep in contact with those on the Curb; in fact, they can be fun, even people you work with. They are not safe people, however. You will do a similar evaluation of people on the Porch, Living Room, or Kitchen, balancing the relationship expectations of the room with the level of trust a person in that room has earned with you. As you work through each room and its inhabitants, you will learn how to be mentally prepared for each person in relationship with you. The more you practice, the easier it gets.

Be Kind to Yourself: You Don't Know What You Don't Know

Please understand—this takes time to master. Once I began understanding where people belonged in the rooms in my house, I had many flashbacks to events I overlooked, comments I accepted, and the passive-aggressive behavior I laughed off.

I was angry at myself for accepting the behavior; I put the people harming me before my own emotional needs. The self-blame and shame I put on myself for not realizing or seeing the signs was embarrassing for me, and I was mad at myself for not being strong enough to say no to the bad behavior.

It is important to hug your past self and say, "You are okay, and you know better now. You will not allow your emotional needs to be second again. You must forgive yourself and move past the behavior of the other person. This is not your fault—you are strong enough, and you didn't know any better, but you will now, and that's what you need to move forward."

Something to remember because I don't want you to think this is all on you: You don't know what you don't know. A person who has never learned boundaries as a child may struggle with friendships in various ways. For example, you might have difficulty saying no to social invitations or requests from friends, leading to feelings of being overwhelmed and overcommitted.

Have you ever felt tired after spending time with certain people? Chances are, they are depleting your emotional energy. You may also have a tendency to overshare personal information or become overly involved in friends' lives; this would be a version of codependency, potentially leading to a lack of privacy and emotional boundaries. You probably began to judge certain decisions you were once sure of and lose a sense of self.

Without a clear understanding of who belongs in the Rooms of Your House, you may have challenges in recognizing and addressing unhealthy behaviors in your friendships, such as manipulation or disrespect. Overall, the lack of boundaries could result in difficulties in maintaining balanced, respectful, and mutually fulfilling friendships.

In my journey of self-discovery, I once believed I was alone in my confusion, thinking that my entire life should be an open book to all. I mistakenly thought that every detail should be shared with anyone who crossed my threshold, whether they were in my Kitchen sharing my hopes and dreams or lounging in my Living Room where we discussed personal information and goals. However, with time and reflection, I came to understand the importance of boundaries, realizing that not everyone is entitled to know every aspect of my life.

I discovered that there are many people, like me, who were never taught the necessity of setting limits. There are also those who recognize the need for boundaries but are uncertain about how to establish them. Others find it challenging to maintain boundaries due to resistance from others.

A profound emotion that often keeps us from asserting our personal space is shame. It can keep us in darkness, making us believe we are undeserving of setting limits. Yet, when we muster the courage to take that step and do something for ourselves, we come to a powerful realization: We are indeed worthy of respect. It is this newfound belief in our own value that illuminates our path to healthier relationships and a more balanced life. We feel empowered to create more boundaries, which leads us to move past emotional blocks and hidden obstacles to achieve our dreams.

It took me years longer than it should have to finally have the courage to say something was wrong. I didn't know what it was or how to fix it, but I knew that I should not be feeling this way. My hope for you is that learning this concept will change the course of your friendships, giving you the know-how and principles to keep and maintain healthy relationships with everyone in your life.

> After college, our son obtained his master's degree and earned his Series 7 license, becoming a financial advisor.
>
> "Are you sure you want to be a financial advisor? You are so young; no one will want you to handle their money," people would say to him. He needed to create boundaries

THE ROOMS IN YOUR HOUSE | 19

with individuals he had known for a long time, and they did push back. Within five years, he became a partner, and only then did he start to receive affirmations and praise.

This was not the first time he had to establish strong boundaries, but from my perspective, it was the first time he faced significant resistance. Eventually, he decided to leave his very comfortable job because it was not personally fulfilling his soul. Despite just purchasing his first house and after one year of being a partner, he saved up a year's salary and quit to find his purpose. It was at this time in his life that he received the most pushback and resistance. I have to admit, even I was asking, "You need to get another job before you quit. Do you have a plan?"

As the one person who should be unconditionally supportive, I found myself questioning him out of love and concern. But once he set boundaries with me and said, "Mom, I love you, but you're done. I'm grown," I had to sit back and watch the struggles that come with starting a business.

Resistance and pushback come in many forms and from many people. Know their hearts, and if they respect your boundaries, they may push back, but if they don't accept your boundaries, you must decide which room they belong in—even a mom like me.

You will be happy to know that was several years ago, and now he owns the largest content house for keynote speakers. Know your worth and understand that you will get pushback. Do it anyway.

Boundaries will be hard; you will get pushback from those you are creating boundaries with, and they will be confused as to why you are being stern. You will need to make it clear you are changing and you are different. Take this as a compliment—you are becoming the person you are meant to be. This means no more open emotional wounds to cover up and, most of all, peace in your heart.

Welcome to the beginning of a new perspective on relationships!

We will be going through each room in the house and how each serves as a "waystation" for the people in your life, all depending on the level of trust you've developed with them. Before we even step inside the house, however, we need to visit the Curb.

Rooms in Your House
Current Relationships

CHAPTER 2

The Curb

Picture your life as a house with various rooms, each representing a different level of trust. In the very front, at the Curb of our house, is where we cautiously start our journey with new acquaintances. It's the furthest point from our inner sanctum, where we share our deepest hopes, dreams, and personal details.

Here, we cautiously place individuals we've just met, those who have not yet earned our trust, and those who may have betrayed us or hindered our personal growth in the past.

The Curb is not a room but a starting point. It's a crucial exercise to begin every new relationship here, and as you read this book, you'll have the opportunity to reevaluate where your current relationships stand.

Everyone starts here—they may not stay on the Curb long, but all must start here because we have just met them, and they have not revealed their true selves yet. As we cautiously navigate the rooms of our relational house, the Curb serves its purpose as a necessary boundary.

It's a space where we can interact with new acquaintances and assess whether they are worthy of further trust, and here is where we can take the time to get to know them and their behaviors. The Curb is where we exercise caution, choosing not to divulge the intimate details of our lives.

Instead, we share just enough to maintain a polite, social interaction. The Curb can be a permanent place for some; however, it is designed to be a transition zone where time and experience will determine if a person can be invited deeper into our personal space—or if they should remain at a distance, safeguarding our inner thoughts and feelings.

This initial placement ensures that everyone begins on equal footing, providing you with a safe space to honestly assess the status of your relationships throughout your boundaries journey.

The concept of the Curb, as I introduced in the first chapter, was born from my personal struggles and years of research, and I want you to learn from my experiences to skip the *I don't know what I don't know* space and move straight into the *I now know and will have peace within my relationships* space. Not everyone should be privy to your story, dreams, goals, or beliefs from the outset, but at the same time, they don't warrant being entirely removed from your life. Thus, the Curb serves as a neutral starting point.

A Note about Our Responsibility

It's crucial, however, to remember that the dynamics of any relationship are not solely about the other person's actions or trustworthiness. We are active participants, too, and our own behaviors, limitations, and boundaries—or sometimes the lack thereof—play a significant role in how our relationships unfold.

By exploring the relational Rooms in Your House, you also gain insight into your contributions to each relationship. Are you, perhaps unintentionally, encouraging a lack of boundaries? For instance, if you find yourself frequently upset because a friend cancels plans at the last minute, consider whether you've communicated how important punctuality and reliability are to you.

> When my daughter was in middle school, she would come home as all young girls do, mention a name and say, "We are beefing." I would then ask, "Do THEY know you are beefing?" To which she would quickly respond no. Okay, then, when you are ready, you may want to talk with them.

If you haven't set clear expectations, your friend may not realize they're crossing a boundary, leading to a cycle of misunderstanding and disappointment. Understanding your role helps you foster healthier relationships where both parties respect each other's boundaries and contribute to a mutual sense of trust.

The concepts of projection and personal boundaries are critical in understanding how your own participation might be contributing to issues in relationships. Projection is a defense mechanism in which people attribute characteristics they find unacceptable in themselves to other people. For example, if someone is uncomfortable with their own anger, they may perceive others as unnecessarily angry or hostile. In this way, they might misinterpret a friend's passionate discourse as an attack when, in fact, it's their own discomfort with conflict that is coloring the interaction.

Another psychological factor is the establishment and maintenance of personal boundaries. If an individual has not clearly defined or communicated their boundaries, they might feel that others are taking advantage of them, when in reality, it's their lack of clarity that has led to the situation. For instance, if you're someone who has trouble saying no and consistently overcommits to helping others, you might eventually feel resentful toward those you're helping. However, from their perspective, they might simply believe you're happy to assist since you've never indicated otherwise.

Additionally, the concept of self-fulfilling prophecy can play a role in how our behavior affects relationships. This happens when an individual's expectations or beliefs about a situation influences their behavior in such a way that it brings about the expected outcome. For example, if you expect that a new acquaintance will eventually betray your trust, you might unconsciously act distant or suspicious around them. This behavior can push the other person away or cause them to act defensively, thereby fulfilling your original expectation of betrayal.

We need to own our part in the relationship as well and understanding these psychological dynamics can help us reflect on our role in relationship problems. By acknowledging our own contribution to misunderstandings or conflicts, it becomes possible to take steps toward healthier interactions, such as improving communication, setting clear boundaries, and challenging our own assumptions and expectations. Open communication and the reality of owning your part in the relationship will set you up for relationship success.

What Kind of Friend Are You? Understanding Attachment Styles

I cannot express enough the importance of this next part for the *Rooms in Your House*—knowing what type of a friend you are and what type of a friend you need. We connect with our friends through shared activities, conversations, needing support or encouragement, and shared interests. We look for the same humor, we want to be vulnerable with someone, and we desire regular communication. That's a lot to ask of someone, but honestly, this is what we as humans need from each other.

It is human instinct to want a friend group and to build connections, which reduces stress and, let's face it, improves overall well-being. If your close inner circle (Living Room or Kitchen) friends are not providing this type of connection, it's time to reassess the friends in your life and learn what type of friend you are looking for.

Some of us value loyalty in a friend, while others want someone to hang out with and have fun. Thrill seekers may want a like-minded friend to go on adventures with, while others want more of a connection to have that special friend they can call several times a day. Maybe you are the friend who needs someone to call once every couple of months.

Knowing what you want in a friend and what you are emotionally able to offer in return will help you build the kind of friendships that truly fit your life. If you have a friend who only sees you through the lens of their own needs—calling only when they want advice—it can lead to a one-sided friendship, which is emotionally draining. By understanding what you need in a friendship and what you're willing to offer, you'll feel empowered to set boundaries and avoid accepting undesirable behavior. This clarity allows you to cultivate the positive, supportive connections that bring peace and joy, while building stronger, more meaningful friendships.

All of us have what are called *attachment styles*, which are the connection styles we use to approach relationships. There are three attachment styles: *anxious*, *avoidant*, and *secure*. Based on how our primary caregivers acted toward our psychological and physical needs in our formative years, we formed an attachment style that reflects that experience. While attachment styles are complex and can vary greatly, this brief explanation is meant to provide a basic understanding, not to serve as a substitute for therapy or in-depth research.

Anxious

Often worries about the security of the friendship; may frequently seek reassurance, checking in to make sure everything is okay. If you don't respond right away, they may think, "Did I do something wrong?"

Avoidant

May feel uncomfortable with too much closeness; value independence and may back away if they feel their friend is too clingy to maintain autonomy.

Secure

The type of friend we strive to be; they can set appropriate boundaries, are safe and stable, and are able to regulate emotions and establish meaningful friendships.

Be observant of behaviors and pay attention to how potential friends communicate. Are they reaching out more frequently than you prefer or not enough? Or do they seem more reserved, and you are more extroverted? This can help you gauge compatibility.

Let's be real—not one single friend can meet your needs or expectations, and you know a diverse group of friends will make you a better person. Building relationships requires you to be aware and honest with yourself and your friends. Just because you have known someone for a long time or they are family does not mean they are the right friend for you. It's okay to not want certain people in your life.

We don't stay one attachment style our entire life; as we develop new ways of managing through different stages of our lives, we learn more about ourselves, how we interact with others, and what our place is in this world. Understanding your own attachment style and the attachment styles of others will help you determine a good fit for the friendships you need in each season of your life.

For a deeper dive into attachment styles, visit www.wendyknipp.com/attachment for a free PDF on Friendship Attachment Styles.

Family on the Curb

The Curb is where everyone starts and where those we are unable to remove from our lives will stay. This is not going to be a popular opinion, however, it needs to be said. For those who have friends or family members who actively betray, abuse, or sabotage you, they should be on your Curb *only* if you feel they need to be in your life.

Even as I write this, it seems harsh to say that some people are at the Curb; therefore, this is a good time to explain why I believe it's important to keep the Curb as a room in my house.

> I was sitting at an outside restaurant bar watching the ocean waves when the two ladies next to me struck up a conversation. I've been told I'm approachable, and it quickly turned into a discussion about creating boundaries within the family. One of them had a brother who had chosen to approach life as the victim, and while the other friend had offered support, her brother had chosen to remain in that role. She hadn't given up on her brother but did limit her time and was no longer easily accessible to him.
>
> The other friend quickly replied, "But he's your brother."
>
> "I understand," she said, "but he doesn't want help, and his negativity affects my mental health."
>
> "But it's your brother; he's family—you can't ignore him."

I share this story because I believe we are still using the idea of family as a reason to avoid creating boundaries, thinking that, because they are family, we are not allowed to protect our own mental health. This is simply not true. We cannot help those who are unwilling to help themselves.

Emotionally, constant exposure to negativity and stress can lead to burnout and resentment, which can poison relationships over time. Motivationally, setting boundaries can actually be an act of self-preservation and self-respect. It allows us to maintain our own mental health and well-being, which is crucial for being able to support others effectively.

Recognize that having boundaries with family members is not only okay but necessary for your well-being. Family members do not need to be in the Kitchen because society dictates we should excuse bad behavior from family. If their behavior warrants the Curb, then to the Curb they go without shame or guilt. I said what I said.

Furthermore, the concept of "family obligation" can sometimes be used to shame us into maintaining unhealthy relationships. However, psychological research supports the idea that setting boundaries is a healthy practice. Referring to practicing boundary skills, Henry Cloud and John Townsend state: "In addition to practicing new skills in safe situations, avoid hurtful situations. When you are in the beginning stages of recovery, you need to avoid people who have abused and controlled you in the past."[4] Boundaries help define where one person ends and another begins, allowing for emotional safety and personal integrity. It's not about abandoning family; it's about engaging with them in a way that is respectful to both parties' needs and limits.

Shaming others for setting boundaries invalidates the person's right to take care of themselves and can perpetuate a cycle of guilt and obligation. It's crucial to understand that setting boundaries is a form of self-care and is a responsible and mature way of managing your relationships, even with family.

I needed a reminder when I walk into a room with them that they belong at the Curb—the space that allows me to protect my heart.

---

[4] Henry Cloud and John Townsend, *Boundaries: When to Say Yes, When to Say No to Take Control of Your Life* (Grand Rapids, MI: Zondervan, 1992), 140.

Not everyone needs access to the inner parts of me, especially if trust hasn't been built. What you have to share with the world is valuable and deserves to be treated with care and respect. Surround yourself with people who uplift and honor that, knowing that your heart is always worth protecting.

Co-workers on the Curb

This principle also extends to business associates who might quickly become friends due to shared interests and common frustrations. Sometimes, we find ourselves in situations where we must work with these individuals. It's like being trapped in a room with a mosquito—irritating, yet you can't simply swat it away.

These challenging associates can range from family members to professional contacts. I will delve deeper into the nuances of workplace relationships in Chapter Six: "The Rooms at Work." For now, you might be wondering: Why would anyone continue to do business with someone who has betrayed or sabotaged them? To illustrate, let's meet Bob.

> Bob is a coworker with whom you've begun to build trust. You've worked alongside him for some time, and he's proven to be a team player. You've come to rely on him; he supports you in meetings and has steered clear of gossip and negative office politics.
>
> At conferences, he has demonstrated respect and upheld excellent standards to the point where you

feel comfortable enough that you've started sharing your professional aspirations with him, enjoyed meals together during these events, and feel that the Porch would be an appropriate place for Bob. He is kind and respectful, and you enjoy his company.

To get to know him socially, you invite him and his spouse to dinner with your significant other. At the dinner, you meet Bob's significant other, Karen. From the outset, she's inquisitive about the rest of the team, inquiring about their salaries and work ethic and proceeds to divulge all that Bob has said about his co-workers. She shares information that should remain private—clearly, conversations meant for spouses alone.

While gossiping with Karen may seem harmless at the moment, her poor discretion and boundary issues potentially undermine your working relationship with Bob. Perhaps Karen is attempting to forge a premature intimacy with the group, but regardless, her actions reflect a lack of boundaries. Since you've just met her, she belongs at the Curb.

Now, considering Bob confides in Karen, and she's privy to his workplace discussions, you realize the need for firmer boundaries. Bob, by association, has moved from the Porch back to the Curb alongside Karen. It's unfortunate—you genuinely like him and considered Bob to be a friend. However, you now understand the necessity of keeping your interactions with Bob strictly professional and maintaining only casual conversations with Karen. Bob shares everything with his wife (nothing inherently wrong with this), but you must be cautious to ensure that nothing you say becomes common knowledge.

This scenario expresses the importance of progressing relationships cautiously. Imagine if you had confided workplace grievances to Bob, who then relayed them to Karen. Maybe even moved him to the Porch without meeting his wife first; knowing what you now know, you would have suffered relationship damage. Given her conduct, she might have spread that information further, either directly to the individual concerned or at the next company gathering. In such a case, the focus wouldn't be on Karen's indiscretion but rather on the content of what you shared.

Don't worry, though; Bob and Karen have the potential to move away from the Curb. This is the beginning of the relationship, and Karen has the potential of self-awareness, becoming someone we can trust. They'll need to demonstrate that they can respect and maintain good boundaries. We'll explore how people like Bob and Karen can move to a different room.

For now, it is important to limit interactions with them. Keeping conversations superficial and protecting yourself from their negative influence is critical to building a strong, healthy relationship with people like Bob and Karen. Understand this does take time, and you will need to keep walls up until you are able to trust them.

Getting to the Root of Curb Behavior

Let's take a moment to consider Karen's social dynamics; in other words, why would Karen behave the way she does and share information Bob shared with her? After all, she barely knows you. You've come to realize that Karen is socially awkward and may not be fully aware of the implications of her actions. While there is room to grace her in if she course-corrects her actions, however, Karen's lack of discretion is an issue because it leads to the inadvertent betrayal of trust. Extending grace to someone is commendable, yet in Karen's case, it's a delicate matter.

Even though you know why she behaves as she does until Karen shows signs of her behavior changing, the risk of betrayal becomes greater when you allow yourself to be open with her. She may not be conscious of the breach of trust her actions cause, which means it's crucial for you not to provide any sensitive information that could be disclosed.

Even though you like Bob, and he has not shown signs of distrust, Bob and Karen are a couple, and it appears that they share intimate details with each other. It's necessary to maintain the same emotional boundaries with both of them.

Gossiping can be a big indicator that someone needs to stay on the Curb, and it really comes down to intent: Are they trying to belittle others or share information in an attempt to discredit the other person? To clarify, when people share private information or talk about others, they might not perceive their behavior as gossip. This tendency often arises from a natural need to connect with others and navigate social landscapes. It makes sense to assume that Karen's sharing of information is driven by such motives, and it's more common than you might think.

Gossip can act as a mechanism for sharing information, helping individuals understand social norms and expectations by discussing the experiences of others. Nonetheless, there's a fine line between innocent conversation and detrimental gossip. Crossing this boundary can have serious repercussions, such as tarnished reputations and eroded trust.

In other words, just because we understand the underlying reasons for certain behaviors doesn't mean we should disregard the warning signs that accompany them. Understanding why someone behaves in a particular way does not excuse their actions, nor does it mitigate the possibility of them betraying our trust. Recognizing the root causes of such behaviors is important, but it doesn't automatically qualify the individual to be welcomed closer into our personal space, such as the Porch or Living Room.

Trust must be earned through consistent, respectful behavior and a demonstrated understanding of boundaries. No one should leave one area of the house to another without first demonstrating the necessary actions required. The more we get to know Karen, the more we realize she was acting out of the need to belong; this is an anxious attachment style, someone who lacks self-esteem, feels less worthy of love, feels others may betray them, and deeply fears abandonment, as we learned about earlier in the chapter.

Why We Gossip

Individuals are social creatures who seek acceptance within their groups and communities. Engaging in gossip can inadvertently become a method to fit in or feel included. Some may not realize the impact of their words, thinking they are merely conversing or exchanging information. Gossiping often serves multiple functions, from bonding with peers to navigating the complex hierarchy of social networks. Moreover, the ease with which people slip into gossip highlights its deep-seated nature in human communication.

Maintaining personal boundaries and working on removing myself from gossip are key practices I strive to uphold. Yet, we often encounter people in our lives who are eager to know the latest news. They might initiate a conversation by disclosing what they've heard, and before we realize it, we're drawn into the discussion.

Imagine you're at lunch with a friend. They begin to talk about their experiences with someone you both know. Internally, you're determined not to engage, but they persist, asking if you've noticed similar things or are privy to certain details. You try to steer the conversation away or dodge the questions, but somehow, the topic resurfaces. Suddenly, they share a scenario that resonates with you, and you think, "I'm not alone in this." That's the moment you find yourself entangled, sharing your own interactions with the person in question, and the cycle of gossip has begun. First of all, we all fall prey to this—I myself, as hard as I work on it, will get sucked in from time to time. The important lesson is that you are self-aware and course-correct quickly.

Gossip, which might seem harmless, can actually mirror deeper social patterns. The reasons behind it—whether it's a longing for connection, a bid for control, or a pursuit of social standing—highlight its dual nature: it can be a social tool but also a source of discord. Therefore, it's important to recognize the unconscious motivations behind gossip to better navigate our interactions and avoid the negative impact it can have on relationships.

It's a common human experience to share stories or information as a way to forge bonds with others, and often, we do so under the assumption that it's harmless. We might think that if we're comfortable with certain details of our lives being shared, then others would be, too, but this is not always the case. This is where the danger lies in confiding in someone like Karen, who may not share the same principles or understanding of discretion. Without a clear sense of personal boundaries, Karen might share information widely without considering the implications.

Karen's seemingly innocent habit of divulging information can quickly undermine the trust others place in her. The willingness to discuss others' private matters without their consent, especially upon a first meeting, is a red flag—it suggests a pattern of behavior that could repeat itself.

Karen, by sharing secrets freely, risks being labeled untrustworthy. While gossip can act as a social glue and a means of circulating information, it can also damage reputations and deteriorate the very foundations of trust in relationships. Karen's desire for connection might be genuine, but without recognizing the potential harm of her gossiping, she may inadvertently sabotage the connections she aims to strengthen. Karen wants to be liked by the group and wants to feel she belongs. I would take a guess, based on my coaching and experience, that Karen does not think about the consequences of her actions. She does not think that by gossiping, she is showing herself as not trustworthy of personal information. We know that if someone is willing to talk to you about others, then they are willing to talk about you to others. It has not occurred to her that this is how others see her. If she did, due to the need to belong, she would not gossip about others.

If you think this is you, don't stress. It's natural to reflect on our experiences and wonder: "I do this"—I share my experiences with my friends. Indeed, sharing is a fundamental human need; it helps us validate our experiences and confirms that we're not alone in facing certain situations. The key difference lies in the intent and the context of the sharing.

When we confide in those we trust—those we allow in our Kitchen—we do so because they understand our character and intentions. They are privy to our innermost thoughts and feelings because they have proven themselves to be trustworthy and empathetic. With them, our approach is not about idle chatter; it's a genuine plea for help: "Can you help me process this?" This kind of sharing is about seeking perspective, support, or advice from someone who cares for our well-being.

In contrast, the type of gossip Karen engages in is transactional and self-serving. It's her intent—she shares not out of a need for emotional support but rather to pull information from others or to entertain. Her actions are not driven by a struggle with the situation but by a desire to know more about those around her, often at the expense of someone else's privacy.

When we are with people in our Kitchen, we can be more vulnerable than those in other rooms; we let our guard down, knowing that our disclosures will be met with understanding and compassion, not judgment or betrayal. This is the essence of a supportive relationship, where we are sharing information to connect and heal rather than harm. Remember, if they are gossiping to you about others, the chances are high they are talking about you too. It's a complex emotion, so let's talk about the difference between gossiping and sharing information.

Sharing information. A primary motivator can be the desire for social connection, where *sharing secrets* may create a sense of intimacy and trust. Additionally, people may gossip as a way of managing their own self-image or to *gain social leverage* by possessing exclusive knowledge. Social awkwardness spurs on sharing too much information, and gossiping can alter perceptions and relationships within groups.

I focus so much on the gossip portion in this section because this is usually where we can get confused about our role. This is where the psychological damage of betrayal is based and where relationships we want to work out don't. We get tricked into falling into the gossip circle and then conflict with our inner self, creating shame around how we are interacting with this person. We stay in a dysfunctional connection because we are unable to release the shame. If this is happening, it may be time to ensure this person is on the Curb or at the first step of your Porch; this will give you the mindset of knowing what you are able to speak with them about next time you meet up, and you can mentally prepare for the interaction.

Habitual gossiping often slips by undetected by the individual spreading it. A person may fall into a *pattern* where the sharing of intimate details of others becomes as routine as their morning coffee. They might not even be aware that they're breaching trust or hurting relationships. It requires a *conscious effort* to monitor and acknowledge these behaviors as they occur.

This is why we need to practice social cues and not share other people's stories—and why removing people from the Rooms in Your House is important.

- Excessive gossiping can lead to a deterioration of trust within a social group, as members become wary of sharing information.
- Individuals known for spreading gossip might become socially isolated as others may begin to avoid them to protect their own reputations.

Personal Repercussions

- People who gossip negatively may experience a decrease in self-esteem, as the act of gossiping can reflect their insecurities.

Here is what you can do: Gaining clarity on one's actions regarding sharing secrets and indulging in gossip is crucial. The first step is recognizing what's often an automatic behavior and then engaging in purposeful self-reflection.

Other Problematic Behaviors to Watch Out For

In addition to gossip, we need to be mindful of behaviors that reveal problematic motives that would keep a person on the Curb indefinitely. These behaviors are symptoms of physical, emotional, or verbal abuse, betrayal of trust, or retaliation.

Allowing Trust to Build over Time

It's crucial not to rush the process of moving people through these spaces because trust is a delicate process that needs time to grow and solidify. Each room represents a deeper level of personal connection and vulnerability, and prematurely elevating someone to a room requiring more trust without the necessary foundation can lead to several potential issues.

When we move someone too quickly into a closer emotional space, we risk basing the relationship on an incomplete understanding of their character and values. Without taking the time to observe their behavior across different contexts and over time, we may miss important cues and warning flags that indicate how they handle confidentiality, loyalty, and respect for boundaries.

If these character traits are not thoroughly vetted, we might find ourselves confiding in someone who is not in a good mental space to handle the responsibility that comes with our trust, leading to breaches of confidence or misunderstandings.

In addition, a relationship that escalates too rapidly may not withstand the pressures of conflict or stress. Trust is often tested during challenging times, and if the foundation isn't strong, the relationship may crumble under pressure. This can result in emotional hurt and the erosion of trust, not only in the relationship but also in our general ability to trust others. It also gives us the opportunity to feel our way in the relationship, how we are interacting with them, and whether we should be adjusting our approach and behavior.

Additionally, when trust is given too hastily, it can create an imbalance in the relationship. One party may feel overwhelmed by the level of connection or expectation placed upon them, which can lead to withdrawal or discomfort. On the other hand, the person who extended trust prematurely may feel exposed and regretful if their openness is not reciprocated or respected. These are signs of attachment styles, which we covered earlier in the chapter.

It's nice when we meet someone new who could be a potential friend we can laugh with, travel, and hang out; however, there is such a thing in relationships as too much too soon. A rushed process can also overlook the natural progression of mutual sharing and bonding, which is essential for a healthy relationship. It allows us to evaluate their attachment style from our own and also helps us see the emotional flags that may come up. Gradually moving from one relational room to another allows both parties to build a series of positive experiences and memories, which act as the glue that holds the relationship together during tough times. Otherwise, there is an uneven balance in the relationship where one feels they are closer than another.

Moving rooms too quickly can create an undeserving trust, which will lead to a disconnection from boundaries. What moves people from one relational room to another too quickly, and why do we need to look for the signs?

Building trust too quickly in personal relationships is often referred to as "rushing trust" or being "overly trusting." It can lead to a situation where trust is given before it's been adequately earned. This can sometimes result in disappointment or feeling betrayed if the trust is not reciprocated or respected. It's important to allow trust to develop over time through consistent actions and communication.

Rushing trust in personal relationships can manifest in various forms listed below; these are some of the more common ones you may know and have experienced but perhaps did not know they had names. It is becoming increasingly common to try and build trust too quickly, and we see this especially in people who have codependency or controlling and narcissistic behavior traits.

Watch for These Red Flags of Rushing Trust

These are some of the trust-rushing behaviors I have experienced in the past, and I had to research why I was feeling awkward around these situations.

The most common is love bombing: This is when one person showers another with excessive affection or gifts. It can be a sign of trying to win over the other person's trust and affection quickly. Some people may interpret this behavior as genuine interest, but it can also be a red flag for manipulative behavior.

Excessive praise: When one person continuously compliments and praises a friend to an extreme degree, which can feel overwhelming or insincere. *"I feel like we are sisters." "You are my best friend." "No one understands me like you."*

Constant communication: A friend insists on being in touch all the time, sending numerous messages throughout the day, or expecting immediate responses to communication. They may say things like, *"Why are you not texting me back?" "You OK? I called you three times today."* This is also an anxious attachment style.

Expensive gifts: Gift-giving is very kind; in fact, it is some people's love language. This can be problematic if they are overly extravagant or frequent, however, especially if the friendship is new and such generosity is not appropriate for the level of intimacy in the friendship.

Rapid intensity: When a person wants to spend an inappropriate amount of time together too soon, pushing for a deep and intense friendship by very quickly creating a sense of intimacy that is not yet natural or established. The anxious attachment style wants to be in communication more often; if you don't create your boundaries when you see the signs, this will lead to your new friend feeling abandoned and that you do not like them.

Pressure for reciprocity: When someone is expecting or subtly demanding the same level of attention, praise, and time investment in return, which can create a sense of obligation or indebtedness.

Signs That It's Not Time to Move Rooms Yet

Pay attention to the following signs.

- When one is opening up and sharing deep personal issues, secrets, or sensitive financial information early in a relationship can be an example of rushing trust.

- The excitement of the friendship causes you to dismiss or ignore early warning signs or gut feelings about a person's behavior because of a strong desire to believe in the trustworthiness of the new partner. Typically, you can feel it before you can articulate it.

- Do not make major life decisions based on the other person's input or suggestion without taking the time to consider if this person has proven themselves to be consistently reliable and trustworthy—remember, they are at your Curb. You save that type of trust for someone in your Kitchen or, depending on the situation, the Living Room.

- Allowing the other person to overstep personal boundaries or feeling pressured to overstep theirs due to a premature sense of trust and wanting to please the other person.

While it's natural to want to trust someone you're developing a relationship with, a balance is necessary to ensure that trust is built on a solid foundation of mutual respect and understanding. This doesn't mean you don't spend time with them, have fun, and enjoy them as friends; it's about protecting your peace and mindset. Here are some examples of how rushing trust might manifest in friendships:

- Declaring someone a best friend immediately after meeting them, without taking the time to truly get to know their character and build a shared history.

- Sharing personal or sensitive information very early in the friendship could potentially be used against you if the friend turns out to be untrustworthy.

- Automatically taking a new friend's side in conflicts or agreeing to help with significant favors without understanding the full context or considering the implications.
- Neglecting long-standing friendships to spend an inordinate amount of time with a new friend, assuming that the new friendship is on an equal footing with those that have been nurtured over many years.

If you feel uncomfortable with how quickly a friendship is progressing, but you ignore those feelings in favor of immediate closeness, this can be a sign of rushing trust. Good friends show trustworthiness through honesty, dependability, and loyalty, traits that usually take time to observe and verify in any relationship.

Not all of these examples need to occur for it to be considered rushing the relationship. If even one of these behaviors is happening and you feel uncomfortable, it's time to evaluate the dynamics of the relationship and consider whether you need to establish additional boundaries.

This would be the time to remind yourself they are on the Curb of your relational house so that you don't divulge too much information too soon. Let's meet Jamie and Alex next, who will model rushing trust in a relationship.

> Jamie is an extroverted person who enjoys being around people who are authentic and share the same interests. Because Jamie is aware of boundaries and understands that not everyone views friendships the same way, she is cautious when meeting new people. So, when Alex entered her life with a burst of enthusiasm and affection, it felt like a breath of fresh air. Alex seemed genuine, with

her own thoughts and opinions. They met at a local book club, and Alex quickly took an interest in Jamie, asking to hang out the very next day.

From the start, Alex was incredibly generous, always complimenting Jamie, offering to buy her coffee, and sending thoughtful texts throughout the day. At first, Jamie was flattered and excited to have made such a caring friend, someone who appeared to want to connect on more than just superficial subjects.

Alex seemed to understand Jamie in a way that no one else had before. Perhaps this was the friend Jamie had been hoping to find and bond with. As the weeks went by, however, Alex's gestures grew more grandiose. Expensive gifts started to appear, from the latest gadgets to concert tickets. With daily calls and texts, Alex was always there, offering a listening ear for every problem, big or small, and insisted on spending every weekend together.

New friendships are fun and exciting, but Jamie realized things were moving too quickly. Jamie began to feel overwhelmed by the intensity of the friendship. It was as if Alex wanted to fast-track their bond, skipping past the usual stages of getting to know each other. Jamie was so caught up in the excitement of having similar views and interests that she didn't notice the signs of love bombing.

Jamie began to notice the amount of time and emotional energy Alex demanded and how her other friendships started to suffer due to this emotional demand. Jamie realized that Alex had moved from the Curb to the Living Room too soon.

It was a wake-up call for Jamie. She realized that the constant attention and gifts weren't just acts of friendship; they were tools Alex used to create a sense of obligation and control. Jamie understood that this was what people referred to as "love bombing," a tactic to gain influence and loyalty quickly without a genuine foundation.

While it was important for Jamie to have an honest conversation with Alex, setting clear boundaries and expressing her discomfort with the pace and intensity of the friendship, Jamie first needed to put Alex in a different relational room, either the Curb or the first step of the Porch so that she could build a relationship on an appropriate amount of trust. This would allow Jamie to mentally slow down the pace and stop sharing too much too soon. It will not be easy, and Alex may feel a shift in the friendship, but it is necessary for Jamie's well-being.

Through this experience, we see the importance of taking things slow in new friendships and being cautious of those who try to rush intimacy instead of focusing on genuine connections. Consider the movie *Failure to Launch* with Sarah Jessica Parker and Matthew McConaughey. In the film, Parker's character explains to the parents of McConaughey's character, whom they are trying to get to move out of their house, that she will simulate intimate experiences to establish a connection. She is simulating a forced connection so that he will feel connected and move on from his current situation.

Whether Alex understands this or not, simulating a connection is exactly what they are doing. Perhaps this is the only way Alex understands how to build friendships, or maybe Alex has not learned about the rooms in her house.

Love bombing in friendships refers to an intense and overwhelming display of affection, attention, and friendship gestures that can seem excessive or disproportionate to the level of intimacy or the duration of the friendship. It typically occurs at the beginning of a new friendship or when a friend is trying to win over or manipulate another person.

We call this trauma bonding, creating codependency, and other types of bonding experiences that create the illusion of healthy bonding. We like these types of people because they validate our need to be accepted. However, this type of behavior can become toxic and codependent.

In Jamie's case, recognizing the red flags of love bombing allowed her to reassess the friendship and take steps to protect her emotional well-being. By setting boundaries and communicating her feelings to Alex, Jamie was able to create a healthier space for themselves and any future relationships.

Let's take a look at what a healthy friendship progression would look like for Jamie and Alex.

Healthy Example

Jamie and Alex meet at a local book club. They discover they have similar tastes in literature and decide to exchange contact information to share book recommendations. This is a secure attachment style.

Week 1: Initial Contact

- Alex sends Jamie a message with a list of book recommendations and asks if Jamie has any favorites to share. They have a pleasant conversation about books and agree to chat again after the next book club meeting.

Week 2: Getting to Know Each Other

- At the next book club, Alex and Jamie sit together and discuss the book being reviewed. Afterward, they grab coffee together to continue their conversation.
- They discuss a variety of topics, discovering mutual interests in hiking and a love for *Gilmore Girls*, but they also respect each other's privacy and don't delve into overly personal subjects.

Week 3: Mutual Interests and Respect

- Alex invites Jamie to join a group hike with a few other friends the following weekend. Alex is interested and appreciates the casual group setting.
- During the hike, everyone has a good time, and Alex and Jamie get to know each other better without any pressure.

Week 4: Balanced Communication

- Alex and Jamie continue to text occasionally, sharing thoughts on books they're reading or upcoming events related to their shared interests.
- They make plans to watch a *Gilmore Girls* marathon together but are both understanding when Jamie has to reschedule due to a prior commitment.

Week 5 and Beyond: Building Trust and Friendship

- Alex and Jamie begin to include each other in various social activities, both one-on-one and in group settings. They respect each other's time and space, making sure not to impose.

- They start to open up about more personal aspects of their lives, but only as much as each is comfortable sharing.
- The friendship grows at a comfortable pace, with both Alex and Jamie contributing to the friendship equally, offering support, and enjoying shared experiences.

This is a basic timeline; not all relationships happen in this time frame, and some may take longer. In this healthy scenario, Alex and Jamie are building a friendship based on common interests, mutual respect, and a comfortable pace of getting to know each other. They communicate openly and respect each other's boundaries, which sets a strong foundation for a lasting and balanced friendship.

On the other hand, here is what a relationship timeline would look like if you were being love bombed or love rushed. Let's break this down so that we can get a better understanding of what this relationship-building could look like.

Imagine that Jamie and Alex recently exchanged contact information and expressed an interest in getting to know each other better. Over the next few days, Alex begins to shower Jamie with attention and gifts.

Unhealthy Example

Week 1: The Onslaught of Attention

- Alex texts Jamie every morning with an effusive "Good morning!" message, followed by compliments and well-wishes for the day.

- Alex insists on paying for lunches and dinners, even when Jamie tries to split the bill or take turns.
- Alex sends Jamie multiple gifts, such as books, a care package, and even a high-end gadget, claiming she just saw it and thought of Jamie.

Week 2: Social Media and Emotional Overload

- Alex frequently comments on and likes all of Jamie's social media posts, often with excessive praise or declarations of friendship.
- Alex starts to share deep personal secrets and emotional burdens with Jamie, creating a sense of premature intimacy.
- Alex expects Jamie to be immediately responsive to messages and calls, expressing disappointment or worry if Jamie takes time to reply.

Week 3: Pressure and Possessiveness

- Alex begins to make plans for future vacations and events far in advance, assuming that Jamie will be available and willing to join.
- Alex shows signs of jealousy when Jamie spends time with other friends and may guilt-trip Jamie for not dedicating enough time to their friendship.
- Alex uses phrases like "You're my best friend" or "Miss you, bestie" to create a sense of special connection despite the friendship still being in its early stages.

It's important for people to set boundaries and communicate openly about their comfort levels in any relationship. The love bomber or an anxious attachment style friend does not allow the other time apart to evaluate the situation: Do they even like them, are they attached to them, or is it the gifts and attention they are providing for them? If someone does not offer you time to evaluate the relationship, this would be a red flag.

If you are like me and wonder why people behave the way they do, here are some examples. Know that there are several reasons why an individual might engage in love bombing in the context of friendships or romantic relationships. It does not excuse the behavior; simply be aware and adjust accordingly.

Reasons for Rushing Trust

Insecurity: A person who feels insecure about themselves or their ability to maintain relationships might use love bombing as a way to quickly secure a strong connection with someone else. This is, on a conscious and subconscious level, done by overwhelming the other person with attention and affection.

Fear of Abandonment: Individuals with a deep-seated fear of abandonment may resort to love bombing as a means to create a strong bond quickly, hoping to avoid potential rejection or loss.

Desire for Control: Love bombing can be a manipulative tactic used by individuals who seek to control or dominate a relationship. By showering the other person with gifts and attention, they may be attempting to create a sense of obligation or guilt, which can then be leveraged to exert control over the individual.

Lack of Boundaries: Some people may not recognize or respect the boundaries of a developing relationship. They might genuinely feel an intense connection and express it through love bombing without understanding that their behavior is overwhelming or inappropriate.

Narcissistic Traits: Individuals with narcissistic traits may use love bombing to feed their ego and sense of self-importance. They enjoy the admiration and dependency that love bombing can create, as it reinforces their desired self-image and power in the relationship.

Modeling Behavior: If a person has observed or experienced love bombing behavior in past relationships or in their family of origin, they may have learned to mimic this behavior, believing it to be a normal way to express affection and establish connections.

Impulsivity: People with impulsive tendencies may engage in love bombing without fully considering the consequences. Their immediate desire to connect and express their feelings can overshadow a more measured approach to relationship-building.

Idealization of Relationships: Some individuals may have an idealized and romanticized view of relationships, leading them to engage in love bombing to quickly match their fantasy of a perfect friendship or romance. They might not recognize the need for a more gradual and authentic development of connection.

It's important to note that love bombing, especially when it is manipulative or controlling, can be a sign of an unhealthy dynamic. I have personally experienced this, and due to my own inability to understand boundaries, these individuals quickly went to my Kitchen, where I would give the impression of connectedness. This is why we make sure the Curb is a great place for people to start. They will stay in this spot regardless of love bombing or a simulated connection.

Why Some People Stay on the Curb

A place on the Curb means the relationship should be built on mutual trust, and until they show we can trust them, we need to make sure they stay here. Some stay because they have betrayed trust and actively work to sabotage work, goals, and achievements. Some stay because, as I described above, they love-bomb us, and some stay because we have not been able to establish or create a bond with them to see whether they should stay or move. There are several reasons individuals stay on the Curb and stay in our lives. Please note that does not mean we trust them with anything personal; we don't confide in or trust them until we can establish trust between us.

1. Instead of removing people from your life, if it is not a repeated betrayal, I feel gracing people in helps us stay humble and self-aware, as I, too, have made mistakes in my life. Ask yourself, "What was going on in their life when the betrayal happened? Was it intentional?" No matter what is happening in their life, it does not excuse abuse.

2. People are capable of growth and if they are willing to grow and put in the work to have a healthy relationship. We don't know what we don't know, and once we know, we must do better.

3. Consider the fact that we were meant to learn something from them. Are we to grow from the experience? Perhaps they are in

our life for a season, and we can learn from them. Personally, the hardest and most rewarding lessons have come from the deepest betrayals and hardest times in my life.

These first chapters of the book have introduced the concept of relational spaces, referred to as the "Rooms in Your House." The journey begins at the Curb, where everyone must remain until they demonstrate trustworthiness. This process requires time, and certain red flags—such as love bombing, gossiping, and poor boundaries—signal that it's not yet time to advance someone to the next room. Recognizing these signs is crucial to prevent oversharing and divulging information prematurely.

I caution you to safeguard your boundaries at this stage, as not everyone operates with a healthy mindset. By doing so, we protect our hearts and avoid the recurrent pain of betrayal that stems from sharing too much of ourselves too soon. This approach also helps to prevent the continual reopening of wounds caused by misplaced trust.

I have learned over the years not to linger too long in the process of evaluating where people belong in my life. If I do, I tend to overanalyze, make excuses, and become entangled in the weeds of dysfunction. Trust me, once you've experienced a level of peace, healthy boundaries, and self-care, you'll feel uneasy and need to move on from this place quickly. Listen to your instincts and move forward.

Before I interact or communicate with someone, I remind myself of the room they occupy in my emotional house. No matter how they present themselves, even if they exhibit positive and seemingly trustworthy behavior, I know which room they're in and adjust the level of detail I share accordingly. I mentally prepare not to over-share and to withhold personal information, whether positive or negative. At this stage, they haven't earned the trust to be privy to such details.

For me, the desire for the relationship to flourish and the feeling of connection are important. I am aware of my enthusiasm, and this self-awareness helps me refrain from sharing prematurely.

We hold back not because we want to be secretive but because we recognize that the other person may not provide the healthy support we need. They might say or do something that triggers us or pushes us away from our goals. Their reaction could be negative and potentially steer us in an undesired direction.

I created the concept of the Curb because it is the furthest point from the house, and I designed it as a reminder to my mind not to divulge too much information prematurely. You may not need the Curb; for you, relationships might begin at the Porch. It's important to recognize that I am an over-sharer by nature, and these relational rooms are necessary for me to manage my boundaries and the information I share.

Someone might stay on the Curb for quite a while or indefinitely. Once a true connection is established with someone who's been on the Curb for a while and built trust with us, we can then move them onto the Porch.

Assessing First Encounters:
Who's Still at the Curb?

CHAPTER 3

The Porch

The Porch—there's something special about this part of a home, isn't there? I find myself drawn to the Porch, where I spend a considerable amount of time. Whether it's a Porch, front entry or a courtyard for you, it represents the transitional space before one enters the home. I've often thought I should have lived in the South, charmed by the idea of neighbors strolling by, exchanging pleasantries, perhaps stopping for a brief, meaningful conversation before continuing on their way.

In the journey of friendship, the Porch is the next significant step. It's the place where I choose to linger when a new friendship begins to feel more secure, where I'm willing to invest more time. The Porch in our house symbolizes this phase of growing trust and respect. Here, we relax a bit more, willing to elevate the friendship to the next "room." While it lacks the intimacy of the Living Room or Kitchen, it's an inviting space to start building the connection.

Picture yourself on a porch swing, sipping a refreshing glass of lemonade, iced tea, or, in my case, a Diet Coke straight from the bottle.

This is my sanctuary for reading, watching the world go by, or simply enjoying the ambiance. And I remember that each year when I was a little girl, we would drive to Tennessee and visit my grandmother, where we would sit on the porch. Each morning, my aunts and uncles would stop by to say hello.

It's in this Porch setting that I might share snippets of my personal interests and hobbies. It's the spot I reserve for those I'm ready to welcome into my time and space, yet not into the fully aware of my private life or my deepest reflections.

The Porch, therefore, is not just a physical structure; it's a symbol of the delicate building of new friendships. It's where boundaries begin to soften, where the laughter is a little louder, and the stories a little more personal. It's the place where we test the waters of vulnerability, offering pieces of ourselves and gauging the response. As we sit, sharing the moment, we're also subtly deciding whether to invite our new acquaintances to step through the front door into more personal spaces of our emotional home. It's a beautiful, hopeful stage of connection, filled with potential and the promise of deeper bonds to develop.

This represents a transitionary zone where you decide how much to share with others. Adequate boundaries in this area can shield from being emotionally drained and provide control over the influx of information.

On my Porch, visitors represent varying degrees of intimacy. Some may not intentionally undermine my efforts, yet their support is passive at best. As I get to know them and enjoy their company, I tread cautiously, mindful of past experiences where trust was misplaced.

Three Levels of the Porch

Consequently, I've established on the Porch a sort of three steps of friendship levels, which you might find helpful when assessing your Porch friends. One level may suffice for some, ushering them directly into the Living Room of closeness. The beauty of these relational rooms lies in the control they offer over the depth of intimacy, allowing you to dictate the pace at which you want to be connected with the possibility of moving into the Living Room.

This tiered approach is what works for me, serving as a framework to uphold healthy boundaries. You may find that two levels or even one works best for you. It's essential to determine what feels right for you and your mental well-being. I break them up because I have experienced over the years that some people are *fun friends,* and either they or I feel this is the best level of closeness. Some want friends who are concerned about them; however, they are unable to reciprocate at this time in their lives. Understanding where others are is necessary to establish our rooms.

The **first level** is reserved for acquaintances who bring joy and fun—I feel good around them. The **second level** is for those with whom I share details of my current life but not my past—those stories are reserved for a select few. The **third level** is the inner sanctum of my Porch, where I confide my aspirations. Here, I pay close attention to the dynamics of sharing: Are my new friends actively listening and reciprocating? This is where we listen and watch actions, as some people's actions do not match words. They will say one thing and do another. Do they remember our last conversation? In other words, are they listening to understand or react to what I am saying?

> *Porch Level 1* – for fun acquaintances we feel good around
>
> *Porch Level 2* – share details of current life, but not the past
>
> *Porch Level 3* – the inner sanctum of the Porch, where we confide aspirations (not as vulnerable as the Living Room)

This is also where I am listening to their stories, noticing what types of conversations we are having, for example, and observing whether they are asking about my personal life; inquiring about my personal life too soon can be a sign they want to trauma bond. Are they being overly kind, agreeing with everything and wanting to make plans with me before the current interaction is over? That could be love bombing.

Not everyone will need to start at the first tier for me; it's a personal gauge to determine how much I share during interactions. You may find that they have demonstrated healthy boundaries, and you might feel that the first two steps aren't necessary. However, it's still wise they remain on the Porch until enough time has passed for you to understand their boundaries.

Building relationships takes time; we shouldn't rush the process. We want the relationship to develop naturally over time. Let's get to know new friends, Abby and Mary.

Abby and Mary met through a mutual friend, and the second time they met they were able to talk about mutual interests. Abby shared about her medical issues and other things at home she was struggling with—common concerns for women their age—and Mary offered suggestions. Their exchange was light and helpful, and they connected.

A couple of days later, Abby followed up with Mary, expressing gratitude for the recommendations, which proved to be helpful. Mary then suggested they meet again for coffee. When they reconvened, their conversation was a light catch-up from last time, with a follow-up on furthering that discussion. Mary paid close attention to Abby's responses to ensure she was comfortable with the conversation's direction. She asked follow-up questions and showed genuine interest in Abby's life.

While they touched on some controversial topics, the discussions were welcomed without judgment. At the end of the meeting, which lasted a couple of hours, Abby and Mary felt refreshed, with high energy resulting from a mutual enjoyment of the conversation.

Notably, Abby and Mary refrained from discussing their mutual friend or engaging in gossip about other friends in their group. There was no negative tone, nor was advice expected to be given. When their time was up, Abby felt good about meeting with Mary. Everything had gone well, and they both felt safe, with no yellow or red flags.

This is a great example of a secure attachment style from both Abby and Mary. It's important for Abby to recognize that trust is built over time and through consistent, positive interactions with boundaries and trust. While the temptation to skip ahead to deeper levels of connection is understandable, it's important for her to maintain boundaries appropriate to the stage of their friendship. For Abby, Mary will remain on the Porch of her house—a space where they can continue to enjoy each other's company while still being mindful not to share too much too soon. They will avoid discussing mutual friends and remain diligent about where their friendship stands, recognizing that a strong foundation takes time.

What would happen if Abby and Mary's friendships took a bit of a turn? Maybe Abby was a confidant for Mary but noticed when she needed some advice, Mary did not have the time. Or Abby shared concerns about her life, but Mary never asked how she was doing. From my perspective, a friend is someone who is attentive and supportive not only during the conversation but later on. They are clearly not required to have a vested interest in me; however, if they require it from me, asking me why I didn't ask them about their kids, how their day was, or that it was a hard day, then we have an unbalanced relationship.

So how would I approach this friend? They would stay on my Porch because they require more from me than they are willing to give. I will also consider that perhaps they don't have it in them to give more, and that's OK, but now I need to be aware so that I do not fall for the false idea we are close friends.

In this scenario, it will drain the social energy from one person; they will begin to distance themselves while the other person is left wondering what is happening. It offers peace to both when we understand where each person stands in our lives. Of course, they will think we are connected more than we are because I am offering what they require from a friend; in other words, I am filling their emotional needs, but they are not filling mine.

I am now aware that I need to create boundaries if I want to remain friends with them. Otherwise, they will drain me, and I will become anxious when I interact with them. We may not realize we are feeling anxious; perhaps we are learning about the rooms or boundaries. Assuming everyone is our friend, we would not come to the realization it's the other person's lack of boundaries and invest our time and energy being a Living Room friend when we should have realized it was a Porch friend.

Over time, I will stop asking specific questions that one would ask a close friend to protect my boundaries. Another thing to consider is if they do not participate in asking questions or remember your concerns, perhaps you are moving too fast, or they are not ready for a closer relationship. That's what's nice about Rooms in Your House— you can take it slow enough to protect boundaries.

Keeping the Emotional Balance on the Porch

It's also crucial to remain aware of the balance in our exchanges. Am I revealing more than they are? The goal is to ensure a mutual exchange, to avoid overwhelming them or coming on too strong. After all, we're all at different stages emotionally, and recognizing this helps maintain a harmonious balance in our relationships. We don't want to love-bomb them.

Emotional balance on the Porch is a delicate dance. It's about finding that sweet spot where both parties feel comfortable and engaged. The goal is to foster a reciprocal relationship where the give-and-take of personal stories and support feels natural and equal. It's about ensuring that the emotional investment is mutual and that neither person feels overburdened or underappreciated.

As we navigate these levels of intimacy, it's important to remember that it's okay for people to remain on different steps of the Porch. Not everyone will or should enter the personal rooms of our lives. Each person's presence serves a unique purpose and adds value in different ways. Some may be the sunshine of a casual chat, while others might be the pillars of deep, unwavering support.

Ultimately, the Porch is a place of potential—a space where relationships can bloom in their own time and on their own terms. It's where we learn about others and, in turn, about ourselves. By respecting our own boundaries and recognizing the boundaries of others, we create a welcoming space on the Porch that honors both our need for connection and our need for personal space.

The Porch as a Crossroads

The Porch represents a space of increased familiarity compared to the Curb, yet it still maintains a level of distance and caution. This can be a transitional zone where relationships are more personal than those with strangers or acquaintances but not as intimate as those we invite into our Living Rooms or Kitchens.

The Porch can also represent a transition area for relationships that have not yet had the opportunity to deepen. Some individuals may linger here longer than others, such as a friend from church, a class, or a book club or met through a mutual friend. You may share weekly interactions and a few personal exchanges, but outside of this context, you've only met a handful of times. While there's a sense of connection and a desire to share more, it's important to allow time to observe how the relationship unfolds in different environments.

There are also those who find a comfortable spot on the Porch because they embody the "fun friend" role—the ones you call for a dinner out or the partners of your spouse's friends. These are the people you enjoy being around for specific activities, yet beyond that shared interest, there isn't a deeper personal link. They are wonderful companions in those moments, but the connection doesn't extend far beyond that shared experience.

It's important to recognize these relationships for what they are: enjoyable and valuable in their own right, but not necessarily the ones you would turn to for deeper emotional support. These are also the colleagues who transition into after-work friends, where the connection is friendly and valued yet primarily anchored in the shared experience of the workplace.

While the talk is friendly and the laughter genuine, in the beginning, it steers clear of overly personal topics such as work stresses or family issues.

The Porch stands as a comfortable middle ground, a place where social ties bind us in the spirit of camaraderie, yet an unspoken pact exists to savor the present without delving too deeply into private matters.

Here, we encounter individuals with their own aspirations and life philosophies, engaging in light-hearted discussions about leisure activities and everyday experiences. These exchanges, while not deeply personal, are nonetheless enriching, offering us a window into different perspectives and ways of life that we respect and are curious about.

Marcus Aurelius once remarked, "Humans have come into being for the sake of each other, so either teach them or learn to bear with them."[5] Leviticus 19:18 says, "Do not seek revenge or bear a grudge against anyone among your people, but love your neighbor as yourself. I am the LORD." These sentiments aptly capture the essence of the Porch dynamic.

We are at a crossroads of sorts, where we either invite someone into the more intimate spaces of our lives, gently set the relationship aside, or simply appreciate the connection for what it is without the

---

[5] Jacob Needleman and John P. Piazza, *The Essential Marcus Aurelius* (New York: Penguin, 2008), 66.

expectation of a deeper bond. The beauty of this approach lies in the recognition that not everyone must be a confidant or a close friend. Just as a house is divided into rooms for different purposes, so too are our relationships categorized, allowing us to cherish each person's presence in our lives for the unique role they play.

You see, not everyone wants a deep personal relationship with everyone; in fact, it would be exhausting to only have deep conversations. We need to enjoy, like, and appreciate others for who they are and expand our worldview.

Within the confines of the Porch, I aim to grasp their principles, learn what they hold dear, and watch how they engage with the broader world. This room is perfectly suited for those who might currently lack the bandwidth for more profound connections or for individuals like me who enjoy deeper conversations that may not align with their conversational comfort zones. They might be dealing with their own complexities, opting for more superficial social exchanges, or perhaps they find pleasure in my outgoing personality and the vibrancy it brings. I'm told I am fun! I guess I am sometimes, but being a libra, I have two sides, very serious and a little sillier side. I wish I had a middle ground, but nope. This is me. Some people understand and appreciate, while others end up frustrated and confused.

Within the confines of the Porch, there's a mutual respect for our differences; our shared goal is to savor the pleasantries of our interactions. It's essential to acknowledge that friends we keep on the Porch may not always be adept at handling sensitive information or honoring personal boundaries. This isn't to say they don't have boundaries of their own; rather, they might not share the same level of consideration as yours. They may not prioritize discretion as much and could, even without malice, divulge your private information to others. Conversely, you may be someone who holds secrets too closely, which can be overwhelming for them to handle.

Neither approach is inherently wrong—it's a matter of recognizing and respecting the boundaries that are important to you and discerning which relational room best fits each person in your life.

The Porch Isn't Always Permanent

As with all spaces in this house, residency on the Porch isn't always permanent. Views can change for either friend, or life's journey might lead you both in a new, shared direction. The adage "Some people come into your life for a reason, a season, or a lifetime," though its original author is uncertain, captures the transient nature of many relationships.

The essence of this saying is that not every friendship is destined for permanence; some serve to impart lessons, others are fleeting, and a select few endure alongside us through life's journey. It's in this space that I witness friendships either persist on the Porch or exit from my life, with fewer advancing to the Living Room as I age.

It's important to recognize that growth occurs at varying paces and times, and sometimes, our paths diverge due to changes in beliefs or professional perspectives. There's no necessity for fault or guilt; relationships evolve as they will. The key is to embrace the wisdom gained from each encounter and move forward.

While on the Porch, I exercise caution in divulging sensitive details or delving into profound ideological debates. The requisite trust for such exchanges has not yet been established. We might still be unaware of each other's political or religious stances or whether they are even open to such discussions. It is not necessary, nor is it typically feasible, for all connections in our lives to be deep and involve sharing personal issues. A diverse social network, composed of varying degrees of closeness and types of relationships, is beneficial for our mental health and social well-being.

We Need All Kinds of Room Friends

Deep connections, such as those represented by the Kitchen, are important as they provide a sense of emotional intimacy, support, and trust. These are the people with whom we share our most personal thoughts, feelings, and experiences. However, not all relationships need to reach this level of depth to be valuable.

Friends who are simply fun to be around are also essential. They might be represented by the "Porch" or "Living Room" in the house. These friends provide opportunities for leisure, laughter, and relaxation, which are important for stress relief and overall happiness.

The Living Room might be for friends who are closer and with whom we share more of our lives, while the Porch could be for those with whom we have a more casual relationship. It's important to have a balance of different types of relationships in our social "house." Each type serves a different purpose.

Porch friends offer companionship and shared interests without the emotional demands of deeper relationships.

It's also important to acknowledge that relationships are not static; they can evolve over time, transitioning between different areas of the house as they grow or as life's circumstances shift. Here on the Porch, it's crucial to recognize the authenticity of our connections. While some individuals may not exude the same level of drive or ambition, their presence can still be enjoyable and emotionally fulfilling. It's a common desire to surround ourselves with people who inspire and motivate us, but it's equally important not to overlook the value of those who provide comfort and emotional support.

If you find that none of your friends are encouraging you to pursue your dreams, it might be worth reevaluating your social circle. However, remember that not everyone in your life is there to push you toward your goals. Friendships fulfill a spectrum of purposes and are not merely transactional.

This is a space where you're likely to share more personal aspects of your life, yet within the safety of established boundaries. It's a formative stage where trust is nurtured, and you carefully consider how much further to open the door to your inner world.

Porch Conversations

You might find yourself discussing recent events in the news or a captivating new book you've encountered. Such conversations can spark engaging exchanges that offer insights into your perspectives without sharing your deepest convictions. People vary in their readiness to disclose their beliefs at this juncture—some may eagerly reveal their stances to gauge compatibility, while others reserve such intimacies for the Kitchen level of friendship. My advice is to tread carefully when it comes to debating these beliefs. From what I've observed, attempting to sway someone's firmly held views often solidifies their stance, potentially causing a rift.

Similarly, if you find yourself on the receiving end of a debate, where your views are challenged or dismissed, it might be a signal to reassess the dynamic of the relationship. While it doesn't necessarily mean relegating someone back to the Curb, it could indicate that they should remain on the Porch for the time being and that certain topics are best avoided.

Understanding where you stand helps in establishing clear boundaries. When you're ready to open up a bit more about your ambitions, here are some conversational avenues you could consider:

- You might express your intention to read more this year or your goal to complete a 5k. These objectives are personal yet not overly private, signaling a growing trust. Seeking their recommendations can also be a subtle way to learn about their interests.

- Alternatively, you could discuss your efforts to enhance your gardening, technology, or marketing skills or mention a home renovation project you're undertaking. Sharing these sorts of endeavors reveals a slice of your life without delving into more sensitive personal challenges.

In other words, the Porch is where you start to share more about your life and who you are, but you're still careful about not revealing anything too personal or sensitive. It's a safe space for testing the waters of deeper friendship. You're mindful of the other person's comfort level as well as your own boundaries. As the relationship progresses and trust is established, you might gradually invite the person into the Living Room of your life, where more personal and meaningful exchanges can take place.

As your relationships deepen and you begin to divulge more personal aspects of your life, it's vital to establish and preserve healthy boundaries to ensure that the relationship remains beneficial and does not impinge on your personal comfort or well-being. The following are additional aspects to consider.

Mutual disclosure is a cornerstone of a balanced relationship. Pay attention to whether the other person reciprocates your openness. A healthy exchange involves a similar level of sharing from both sides. Remember,, avoid relationships that feel disproportionately one-sided, as they may lead to an unhealthy imbalance.

Be cautious of any pressure to divulge more than you're ready to. Your boundaries should be respected, and your shared information should never be used against you. A friend should not coerce you into revealing more than what feels comfortable for you.

Pick up on social cues and strive to understand their personality. The consistency with which they treat you and acknowledge your boundaries is crucial for a relationship to be deemed trustworthy. Trust is built through consistent, respectful interactions that honor each individual's comfort levels.

It's also important to be mindful of how the person responds to your boundaries. A respectful individual will accept and adhere to your limits without making you feel guilty or unreasonable.

Finally, *remember that boundaries can evolve.* As trust grows within a relationship, you might feel more comfortable sharing deeper aspects of your life. However, this should always be at your own pace and on your own terms. It's okay to reevaluate and adjust boundaries as needed. By keeping an eye out for these signs and maintaining a clear sense of your own limits, you can foster relationships that are both fulfilling and respectful of your personal space.

When Trust Is Broken on the Porch

Reassessing the boundaries of a friendship can be a challenging but necessary process. Let's consider a scenario where someone might need to distance themselves, effectively moving a person from the Porch back to the Curb. Meet Mark and John.

> Mark and John hit it off at a local book club, bonding over their love for literature and golfing. Initially, their Porch-level friendship thrived on enthusiastic exchanges about the latest books and the best golf courses. Mark even felt at ease inviting John to join his inner circle for a round of golf.

But the dynamic shifted when John started making jokes at Mark's expense while golfing with other friends. Mark felt it was important to communicate his discomfort, so he addressed the issue with John in private, expressing that the remarks were offensive. John apologized, and Mark, believing in the value of their connection, accepted this apology. However, when John repeated this behavior and went as far as sharing a personal anecdote that Mark had entrusted to him, it became clear that John wasn't respecting Mark's boundaries or the privacy of their conversations.

Recognizing that his trust had been breached, Mark made the difficult decision to dial back their interaction to courteous exchanges during book club encounters, thus moving their relationship back to a Curb level. In doing so, Mark prioritized his own peace and self-respect.

It's important to note that this recalibration of boundaries is a personal and internal decision. Mark wouldn't literally inform John that he's been "moved to the Curb." Such a conversation might not even take place. Instead, Mark would naturally adjust the amount of personal information he shares and the frequency of their interactions. This subtle shift allows Mark to safeguard his emotional well-being while still maintaining a cordial acquaintance with John.

When and How to Communicate Boundaries

There are several reasons Mark might opt not to explicitly inform John of the change in their friendship dynamics, comparable to not disclosing the room he's in or that he's being moved to the Curb: The spaces within your house are symbolic of personal boundaries, serving to safeguard your emotional well-being.

Humans are generally predisposed to avoid conflict and maintain social harmony. Telling someone that they have been moved in terms of friendship levels can lead to uncomfortable confrontations. Mark may prefer to avoid this potential conflict by not explicitly stating the change in their relationship status.

Some individuals are more inclined toward indirect communication styles. Instead of confronting issues head-on, they might opt for more subtle cues to communicate their discomfort or dissatisfaction, hoping the other person will pick up on these signals.

Relationships are complex, and Mark might be unsure about completely closing the door on the friendship. By not categorically stating the change, he leaves room for the possibility of reconciliation or future improvement in the relationship.

It's also a matter of social etiquette. It's the unwritten rule effect—we know it's happening, but no one talks about it. Explicitly telling someone that you're changing how you interact in the friendship is not a common social practice and can be seen as rude or insensitive. It's more socially acceptable to let the relationship fade naturally through less frequent contact and sharing. This is not the same as ghosting—you still have contact, but it's not as frequent and conversations are social.

Mark may anticipate that John, through self-awareness, would recognize his actions that led to a shift in their friendship's dynamic. It is often expected that a person will understand the underlying reasons for a relationship cooling without an overt explanation.

Verbally labeling the stages of a relationship can be counterproductive, potentially introducing unnecessary strain. It can be perceived as a form of social rejection, which might lead to feelings of hurt, confusion, and even shame as one might ponder their perceived shortcomings. Our individual life experiences, social dynamics, and current circumstances shape our perspectives, influencing why someone may "change rooms" in our lives—they may not align with our "tribe," or we may not fit into theirs.

People often intuitively sense changes in a relationship through altered patterns of interaction. You might notice that calls become less frequent, invitations to social events dwindle, or text responses are delayed. These behavioral shifts and subtle cues are common methods of signaling changes in our relationships, allowing them to evolve organically without the need for blunt conversations that could lead to confrontation.

Personal values and priorities vary widely. For instance, while I place high importance on honesty and would prefer my children to be upfront with me—even if the truth is unpleasant—others may accept that children sometimes lie as a part of growing up and testing boundaries.

In fact, when my daughter was younger, after sending her to clean her room, I would go to inspect, asking, "Did you put everything away, or is it all under your bed?" She didn't even try to lie; she just answered matter-of-factly, "It's all under my bed." I loved her honesty. Side note: She is still like that—she will tell the truth because she is not afraid of healthy confrontation.

Boundaries are the personal rules we set for ourselves, and they guide how we expect to be treated by others. However, these boundaries don't always need to be articulated unless they're being crossed. Informing someone about their "room" status is less about maintaining a healthy boundary and more about categorizing the relationship, which can be unnecessary and even harmful.

Those with high emotional intelligence are skilled at navigating the nuances of human relationships. They understand that discussing the status of a relationship outright can be tactless and fail to capture the intricate emotions and connections that are present. They are attuned to the feelings of others and manage relationship dynamics with empathy and care.

In essence, the concept of different rooms in a house serves as a psychological framework for understanding and managing our social connections. It is a tool for internal reflection rather than a blueprint for explicit communication.

Dealing with Betrayal on the Porch

Although this is a space to develop deeper connection, we may need to address when situations arise—not all conflict is negative. Noticing the early signs of betrayal can prevent the deep emotional impacts that come when trust is broken. It's important to be aware of subtle shifts in behavior, respect for privacy, and the integrity of trust that can signal betrayal.

They may begin to act differently around you, exhibiting **new habits** or **attitudes** that feel out of character. For example, a friend might suddenly become more secretive, abrupt, or less inclusive in social settings, indicating that something has shifted in the dynamic of the friendship.

Betrayal may be taking shape if there is an **unwarranted intrusion into one's personal affairs**. This could take the form of a friend reading private messages without consent or discussing personal details about someone with others, breaching confidentiality that was previously respected.

When trust begins to erode, it's often one of the most telltale signs of betrayal. Indicators include **frequent dishonesty, unreliability,** or a friend showing signs they no longer **value the relationship** with the same level of connection. This erosion can manifest as broken promises or consistent letdowns.

Depending on your level of the Porch, this may be a good spot to confront the betrayal. If you feel this is a relationship you want to keep, and depending on the level of betrayal, you can choose to put them at the Curb. Or if you want to continue with the relationship, this would be a good time to have a conversation. As a side note, if someone betrayed or deceived you, it would be a good time to visually put them back on the first step of the Porch or even the Curb. This allows you to take some time to evaluate the behavior. If you feel confronting is appropriate, you have time to gather your thoughts.

Addressing the situation with care is crucial for both personal healing and the future of the relationship, so consider timing when preparing to confront a friend's betrayal. It's advisable to approach the conversation when emotions are settled and both parties are likely to be receptive. Seeking a private and comfortable setting can facilitate a more honest and open dialogue.

Effective communication involves expressing one's feelings without accusation and actively listening to the other person. One should speak in **"I" statements** to convey how the betrayal affected them personally, e.g., "I felt hurt when . . ." This approach encourages the friend to understand the impact of their actions without feeling attacked.

Post-confrontation, it is essential to establish clear **boundaries** to prevent similar issues in the future. This may include:

- **Expectations**: Articulate what is and isn't acceptable in the friendship.
- **Consequences**: Discuss what will happen if the boundaries are not respected.
- **Rebuilding trust**: If the decision is to continue the friendship, define steps on how trust will be rebuilt over time.

It's important to remember that when friends betray someone within an inner circle, the emotional shockwaves can be profound.

This section explores ways in which you can confront these emotions and employ strategies to heal and regain your sense of harmony.

Initially, you must recognize the range of emotions you're experiencing. From a sense of shock to deep sadness, each feeling deserves attention. Journaling is a practical step for managing these intense emotions. Writing can serve as a reflective activity, allowing you to process and understand the full extent of your feelings.

During times of betrayal, reaching out for support from trusted people or professionals is crucial. Friends, family, or therapists can provide a listening ear and guidance. They also help validate feelings and experiences, which is an important aspect of moving forward.

Practicing self-care is fundamental to healing from betrayal. Actions that promote physical and emotional well-being, like exercise, a balanced diet, or meditation, are essential. Gaining resilience can also involve setting boundaries to protect your emotional space. Over time, these practices can fortify your ability to cope with adversity and foster a healthier response to future challenges.

In the aftermath of betrayal, you face a crossroads: to mend the fractured friendship or to part ways. The choice hinges on the relationship's value to those involved and their capacity for forgiveness and healing.

The Importance of Intent

We discussed in detail in a previous chapter the difference between gossip and sharing; here, I would like to mention the importance of intent in a relationship. If the intent behind sharing the story is to inform or seek advice in a respectful manner, it may not be considered gossip. However, if the intent is to spread rumors, entertain at someone else's expense, or malign the mutual friend, it could be seen as gossip. If you find the intent is crossing your core values or in any way not honoring your boundaries, then, my friend, it's at this stage you need to decide whether this individual stays on the Porch and you are guarded, or they are back on the Curb.

What is the intent behind the information being shared? If sharing a story that includes sensitive, private, or potentially embarrassing information about the mutual friend that they wouldn't want to be shared, then the intent is self-serving and should be considered someone that has crossed the boundaries, especially if it's shared outside of a context of trust and confidentiality.

Consideration of how the shared story affects the mutual friend is important. If it has the potential to harm their reputation or relationships, it's more likely to be categorized as gossip.

In essence, the intent behind the actions typically involves unnecessary and potentially harmful talk about someone who is not present, especially if the information is personal, unverified, or shared with a negative intent.

I want to briefly discuss triangulation, or someone who acts as a "splitter." This pattern was significant in my relationships, and it took me a while to recognize its impact. Here's how it typically works: In a friend group of three, there's often one person who takes on the role of organizer or mediator—the one everyone goes to for support or to vent. However, when this person is a "triangular," they're actually instigating drama and tension between the other two.

Here's an example: Imagine you vent to this friend about something that frustrated you with the other person. Perhaps they even initiate the conversation by asking if you found something that happened upsetting. You agree, share your frustrations, and feel understood. But then, unbeknownst to you, this friend reaches out to the person you vented about and shares what you said. This often leaves you feeling vulnerable, thinking, "Why am I so upset? I did say those things, and they're not lying." Yet, there's a feeling of betrayal because of how it's presented.

The twist here is that this friend genuinely craves control and has a deep need to feel important and indispensable in the group. By being the one both friends turn to, they maintain a position of authority and involvement. They don't see themselves as doing anything wrong because, in their mind, they aren't gossiping or fabricating stories—they're merely "sharing the truth." However, the way they encourage and then selectively disclose conversations creates ongoing friction between you and the other friend.

The problem isn't that they're outright lying; it's that they twist the context. They encouraged you to share your frustration, then carefully relayed it in a way that fuels tension. This makes them the person you both rely on, further deepening their sense of control. Meanwhile, the dysfunction continues as they manipulate these dynamics to maintain their position as the one both friends need.

When in Doubt, Trust Your Gut

Recognizing when to adjust boundaries and potentially move someone to a different room in your life often hinges on your emotional responses during and after your interactions with them. If you find yourself feeling consistently unsettled, resistant, or negative around someone, it could be an indication that your boundaries are being challenged or that the relationship is not positively contributing to your well-being.

Sometimes, our gut feelings can signal that something is amiss with someone, even if they are widely admired or liked by others. This intuitive sense might not be immediately explainable but can later be validated as more information comes to light. Trusting your intuition is important, especially if it's a persistent feeling. If you're fortunate enough to have a friend with a keen sense of intuition, valuing and heeding their insights can be beneficial.

Testing boundaries can be as simple as saying "no" to a small request to gauge the other person's respect for your limits. Their reaction can provide insight into how they might handle more significant boundaries. For instance, I once had to assert my need for space to a friend when I felt overextended by our interactions. When I explained that my social battery was low and that I needed some downtime, her understanding and accommodating response—suggesting a low-key movie night instead of a more demanding social activity—reaffirmed the health of our friendship and her respect for my needs. This kind of supportive reaction is a positive sign that the person values your boundaries and is willing to adapt to maintain a comfortable relationship dynamic.

Pay Attention to Your Values

Are your core values in alignment? While you don't need to agree on everything, having a foundation of shared values can help in respecting each other's boundaries.

Perhaps you have friends that you enjoy spending time with; however, they enjoy activities that are out of your comfort zone. You can still hang out, have fun, and excuse yourself and head home when they are ready for more energetic activities. I personally don't like to sit at one location for hours; if we want to continue, then I will suggest a coffee spot or a dessert place.

As previously mentioned, trusting your instincts is key. If you feel uneasy about a relationship, it may be time to reevaluate and consider establishing firmer boundaries.

Navigating a Breach of Your Boundaries

When someone consistently challenges your boundaries or attempts to persuade you to alter them without a valid reason, it's a serious issue. My own experiences have made me particularly vigilant about maintaining my boundaries, but regardless of personal tendencies, it's critical to guard against boundary violations.

As we learned in Chapter 1, setting boundaries is an act of self-respect and is fundamental to any healthy relationship. Being explicit about your boundaries and upholding them is vital. As you navigate the process of sharing yourself with others, remember to keep these boundaries in check and adjust them as necessary to ensure that the relationship remains mutually respectful and enriching.

Joanne, whom I met at a professional event, quickly became a valued friend as we supported each other's aspirations. She stood out in our industry for her integrity, never engaging in gossip, and always keeping confidences secure. At social gatherings where industry secrets were often the currency of conversation, Joanne maintained her discretion, never betraying the trust others placed in her.

Our friendship evolved naturally, moving from a casual acquaintance to a more meaningful connection. We would discuss our professional objectives and occasionally share personal dreams, finding common ground in our core values.

During a period of growing trust, I shared with Joanne that I had never been on a girls' trip, a personal fact I had kept to myself. However, at a subsequent event, Joanne mentioned my lack of this experience to others, which left me feeling exposed and somewhat betrayed. I chose to wait for an appropriate moment to address the issue calmly and directly.

Joanne had been on the verge of becoming one of my closest friends, and this slip-up was unexpected. When we talked about the incident, she expressed sincere regret, acknowledging that she had not grasped the personal nature of what I shared.

Her response to our conversation was compassionate and understanding, emphasizing that everyone's life journey is unique and there's no shame in having different experiences.

By handling the situation with openness and respect for my feelings, Joanne not only reaffirmed her trustworthiness but also demonstrated a deep respect for my boundaries. This incident did not push her away; instead, it brought her closer, as her actions following our discussion showed a commitment to maintaining the trust and respect foundational to our friendship. Joanne's understanding and response to the situation ultimately secured her a place in my Living Room, the innermost circle reserved for my dearest friends.

In illustrating this story of good boundaries with a friend, it's worth suggesting that open communication is key. If a similar situation arises, it's beneficial to clarify which topics are private and which are shareable. This preemptive measure can help avoid misunderstandings and ensure that both parties feel comfortable with the level of personal information being disclosed.

The episode with Joanne highlighted the qualities of a robust and healthy relationship, underscored by candid communication and reciprocal respect. Although I initially felt betrayed, the outcome didn't result in a setback to mere acquaintance status for Joanne. Instead, it solidified her status as a trusted friend, a testament to the critical elements that sustain and deepen trust in any relationship.

Joanne's immediate reaction to my expression of hurt was one of comprehension and regret. She listened intently, validated my feelings, and owned up to her misstep without excuses. This level of accountability is fundamental to respect and is crucial for laying a foundation of trust.

The respectful conversation that ensued provided a path to a positive resolution. We avoided letting the incident widen into a divide, choosing instead to have a frank dialogue that enhanced our understanding of each other's limits and expectations. Joanne's readiness to absorb the lesson and my willingness to forgive and move forward exemplified the emotional maturity in our friendship.

Moreover, Joanne's history of upholding confidentiality and her commitment to not engaging in gossip had firmly positioned her as a trustworthy individual. This consistent demonstration of ethical conduct was significant in ensuring that our friendship remained strong rather than regressing to a less intimate level. This was over fifteen years ago, and we are still friends.

The grace with which Joanne and I navigated this challenge is a testament to the resilience of healthy relationships, which can indeed thrive when both individuals are dedicated to empathy and personal growth. It's through these sensitive moments, handled with care and mutual respect, that we truly gauge the depth of our bonds and the reliability of those we call friends.

Joanne's graceful response to the misunderstanding not only allowed her to retain her place as a trusted friend but also paved the way for her to be welcomed into the closer circle of the Living Room. Conversely, had Joanne reacted defensively or attempted to shame me for feeling upset, it would have been a red flag for potential future issues in our friendship. Such a reaction could have resulted in her being placed on the Curb, as mentioned at the end of the previous chapter. In that space, she would have had to wait while I took time to process the situation or reassess the friendship's dynamics.

Building Trust for the Living Room

Transitioning from the Porch to the Living Room within a relationship is indeed a significant move, signaling a deeper level of trust and comfort. But how do you decide if it's the right time to move someone into the Living Room of your boundaries house?

Consider the developing friendship between Emily and Sarah, who first met at a beach yoga class. Their initial exchanges were courteous and focused on yoga—a classic example of Curb-level interaction. As their acquaintance blossomed, they found themselves engaging in more extensive conversations before and after yoga, stepping onto the Porch of a budding friendship. A shared passion for hiking, the beach, and a healthy lifestyle led them to venture on a day trip together.

During this hike, Emily felt comfortable enough to share her ambition of starting a business, a vision she had kept close to her chest. Sarah reciprocated with attentive listening and by offering insights from her own career shifts, demonstrating sincere interest and encouragement. This mutual exchange marked a pivotal moment—they both recognized a trustworthy and meaningful connection was forming. As time passed, their bond deepened through shared personal endeavors and mutual support during life's fluctuations, comfortably ushering them into the Living Room phase of their friendship, where authenticity and ease prevailed.

Those who have reached the Porch stage have proven their reliability, typically maintained a consistent demeanor, and showed resilience amid stress or change. We want to spend more time with them and start to build a deeper relationship.

Remember back in Chapter One, where we talked about why the rooms were established? We have rooms because we don't want to give too much of ourselves away at one time, leaving us open for intentional or unintentional situations that may come up. We know when we are in the presence of the Porch friend or, to be honest, any room friend—we know where we stand with them and know how much we can reveal.

We know we are in a safe place and that there will be different times when we feel a closer connection than other times. Perhaps we had a life-altering day, we let our guard down, or that one drink with friends turned into several, revealing more of ourselves than we wanted to. We know we are in the transition to the Living Room phase when we feel comfortable with letting our guard down and we are sharing more of who we are to them.

Let's think of this from the friend's perspective: Maybe we do share too much and while we are comfortable with the exchange, the friend is not. They begin to change the dynamics of the relationship and use an avoidant attachment style. They may be thinking, "Too much too soon." That's when you know it's not time to move them to the Living Room.

I have helped my clients navigate through the realization of Porch friends. Things are progressing, and one day, they think the connection is strong. Then, a situation happens that crushes my client. She thought they were Living Room friends but realized her new friend never showed signs of vulnerability or sharing personal information. Her actions showed she wanted to be Porch friends—nothing deep, as she was not in a space to give that type of energy.

That does not mean it is a negative situation for either person. In fact, knowing the rooms our friends are in can help us appreciate them for who they are. No judgment, no disappointment—we are all on a different journey, and we can love them where they are.

I think that is the problem with folks who we want to have friendships with but we keep getting disappointed with their actions. People say, "Don't expect anything, and you won't be disappointed." I think if we understand where they are in which room, we can expect only that and nothing more. Then I believe we are not disappointed. It is not a negative thing that we know where each of our friends stand with us. It actually helps build relationship and offers a new perspective on friendships.

It's essential to observe the emotional responses of Porch friends—this period of growing familiarity is when individuals start to lower their guard. It's often during this time that a person's true nature begins to shine through, as consistent imitation is hard to maintain beyond a few months, based on my observations. Psychological stability is also reflected in a person's ability to handle emotional experiences in a socially appropriate manner, allowing them to stay adaptable and competent across various circumstances.

While spending time on the Porch phase of a relationship, it's crucial to observe whether the other person can recover from setbacks, trauma, or stress—essentially, their capacity for resilience and adaptability in the face of change or challenging circumstances.

Key indicators to watch for include whether they exhibit a relatively stable baseline of behavior and emotional responses across various situations and over time and whether they maintain a balanced and realistic outlook on life. An ideal friend wouldn't swing to extremes of optimism or pessimism but would navigate life's highs and lows in a constructive manner.

A coherent and consistent sense of self is also significant. This stability contributes to a predictable understanding of how they may react in different scenarios and is indicative of a well-integrated personality.

Psychological stability is a vital component of mental health and overall well-being. It's the foundation that allows people to operate effectively in everyday life and to cultivate healthy, enduring relationships. It's essential to recognize that psychological stability doesn't equate to a lack of emotional depth or the suppression of negative feelings. Instead, it refers to the capacity to experience a spectrum of emotions while managing not to be incapacitated by them.

The Porch, in my opinion, is the most important part of the house; this is where actual friendship-building takes place and where we begin to understand why we connect with some over others. I am not a therapist, and it would take much more than this book to understand behaviors and why we attract certain behavior types. If you are struggling—and we all do—with attracting toxic people in your life, I recommend seeing a therapist.

Porch Overview

The Porch sets the tone for a healthy relationship. Setting clear trust boundaries ensures that all parties are aware of the expectations within the friendship.

This includes:

- Outlining what is considered acceptable behavior and what is not
- Regularly revisiting and updating these boundaries as the friendship evolves
- Being aware of what you are disclosing
- Are they keeping your trust?
- Understanding your part in the relationship

These steps can serve as a strong buffer against potential betrayal.

Relationships that typically inhabit this intermediary space might include neighbors with whom we exchange pleasantries but not confidences, work colleagues who share a common interest but not the details of personal life, or perhaps the partners of close friends—people we encounter socially but with whom we do not share a direct bond. These interactions are characterized by a friendly distance, where the warmth of casual conversation prevails over the closeness that invites personal revelation.

The Porch, therefore, is a place of pleasant social exchange and growing connections, as well as a boundary to be navigated with care. It's about striking the right balance between offering a warm welcome and protecting our private realms, which is crucial for cultivating healthy, respectful, and enduring relationships. I will leave you with one last story about knowing you have a Porch friend in transition to a Living Room friend.

Before this day, we only shared social information, what kind of books we liked, movies we had seen, and travel experiences. We touched on our religious views, but until this day, I knew very little about her. While we still need more time to develop our friendship, this is how secure attachment styles interact in building strong, mutual, respectful friendships.

I was recently sitting in a coffee shop where a friend and I were discussing several topics when I noticed the person next to us glancing over. As you know, in this environment, the tables are very close; it's not hard to overhear conversations. Religion was one of the topics he seemed interested in, so I asked if he wanted to join the conversation. As we sat there, I, being Christian, my friend who believes in energy, and our new friend whose religion is

Judaism, found ourselves in one of those rare moments in time where we each had our opinion.

We did not judge the others and, with genuine interest, wanted to discuss the topic of the afterlife. It was clear in that moment that all three of us understood the boundaries we needed to adhere to and respected each opinion without sharing intimate details of ourselves. It was not weird, uncomfortable, and was, in fact, enlightening. As we switched topics over to how different humans view the world, we all agreed that everyone—in the world they are experiencing—is doing the best they can.

I was so invigorated by this three-hour coffee session that I came home and wrote. So, to my friend and my new friend sitting next to us, thank you for filling my emotional bank account.

I am aware these moments are rare, and I appreciate the open dialogue without the judgments and shame because we didn't have the same beliefs as the others. When you feel this kind of energy and feel safe to discuss such topics without judgment or fear of being shamed, you know this is a healthy, secure friend you have built a connection with.

Re-evaluating Proximity:
Porch Friends

CHAPTER 4

The Living Room

Welcome to the Living Room, also known as the family room. Growing up, this was the space where we invited friends over to share time and create memories. In our Living Room, these are the individuals who have earned a place of trust. We have shared mutual experiences, and they offer support, encouragement, and a safe space to share hopes, dreams, and emotions.

The living room has always been a place of connection—a space where family and friends naturally come closer. Growing up, it was where we'd gather, watch movies, and share laughter.

When we sold our family home and moved into a smaller place, we quickly realized how central that room had been to our lives. We ordered a new couch, but it never arrived. For three long months, our living room sat empty, and when our kids came over, the missing couch was a constant reminder of the gatherings I was missing.

Having just left the old furniture store to inquire about our lost couch, we stopped in another store to look around. Walking past a sofa, I sat down, and a rush of emotion came over me. Sitting on it reminded me of all the family movie nights and the laughter that had filled our previous living room. Tears welled up as the memories washed over me. It was much more than a missing couch from our new place—it was the connection I had built with my Living Room friends and my family; I felt safe with them. My husband, Wally, saw how much it meant to me, and being the thoughtful man he is, he arranged for that couch to be delivered that very week.

This experience reminded me that a Living Room should feel like an extension of who you are—a place where you can truly be yourself, surrounded by comfort and warmth. Just as that room brought my family together, I hope you find the same sense of belonging and ease in your own Living Room. It's not just a room; it's a reflection of the relationships that mean the most.

The Living Room in our relational boundaries house represents a space where we gather with others, share our time, and build connections. It's a place of comfort and interaction, but it also needs to be a space where boundaries are respected. Just as we might arrange our Living Room to accommodate different activities and guests, we must also navigate our relationships with an understanding that everyone has different priorities and limits.

How do these individuals get to be in the Living Room? Glad you asked! Some individuals have started at the Curb and moved to the Porch. As discussed, there are three levels on the Porch. Whether they have gone through all three or skipped to the third, they must spend enough time there to build intimacy with clear boundaries.

We Need Living Room People in Our Lives!

It is important to have people in our Living Room to support our emotional health. We want to create a sense of connectedness with others. We need people in our lives who we can trust and rely on because a strong support system is essential for our emotional and mental well-being. Having at least one person we can count on provides several key benefits: We need to accept and offer emotional support, and these trusted individuals can offer comfort during difficult times, helping us navigate through stress, anxiety, and sadness. Their presence alone can be a source of solace. Offering and being provided perspective and advice is sometimes needed and is a much-needed source during a minor crisis. We need an outside perspective to see things more clearly. Trusted friends or family members can provide honest feedback and advice, helping us make better decisions.

Support during Challenges

Belonging to a group offers a support system that can provide help and encouragement during challenging times. This network of support can enhance our resilience and ability to cope with life's difficulties. These are the people we call for advice when facing challenging situations. They are the ones we can say, "I need a few minutes; I'm not in a good space right now," and they will stop what they are doing to be there for us.

Goals & Commitments

We also need trusted people who can help hold us accountable to our goals and commitments. They can encourage us to stay on track and support us in our endeavors; they are in our corner, offering support, not hindering our achievements—they want what's best for us.

Social Interaction, Companionship & Belonging

Human beings are inherently social creatures. Forming deeper connections with others satisfies our innate need for social interaction and companionship, which is essential for our happiness and mental and emotional health. Of course, we need people in our lives who will help us celebrate successes and happy moments. We want others to hype us up and those we trust amplify our joy. Shared experiences create lasting memories and deepen our bond. A strong support system can make us more resilient. Knowing we have someone to turn to in times of need can give us the strength to face challenges head-on. We want to feel like we belong.

In essence, while the size of our support system can vary, the presence of at least one reliable and trustworthy person is invaluable. They help us maintain our mental health, provide guidance, and enrich our lives with meaningful connections.

Finding a Healthy Balance in the Living Room

This is a trusting environment, so we must not take advantage of our friends, nor should we be a burden. Be self-aware of calling upon friends too often, as they also need to maintain their own positivity. We want to share the parts of our lives that are positive and negative;

too much focus on your issues can take a heavy toll on their mental health, potentially triggering or complicating their own struggles.

There comes a point where we need to set boundaries and say, "I feel you need more advice than I can offer right now." We want to trust that when we call upon them, they will listen without judgment and provide an honest opinion based on love. This is crucial when we are overthinking and unable to look at a situation objectively. When they share the truth, we know it comes from a place of love, not judgment. These are people who may stay with us for a while or a lifetime, supporting us. Some may even move to our Kitchen, while others might leave when things get too hard. It's important to note that some people leave not because of you but because they are not in a position to be supportive and may need more support themselves during certain periods in their lives. Remember, everyone has a self-journey that has nothing to do with us.

We must not take advantage of our friends, nor should we be a burden, for several important reasons: Friendships are built on mutual respect and reciprocity. Taking advantage of friends or overburdening them can strain this balance, potentially leading to resentment and weakening the relationship. Everyone has their own challenges and emotional limits. Constantly relying on friends for support without considering their well-being can negatively impact their mental health, as they may already be dealing with their own issues.

Healthy friendships are sustainable when both parties feel valued and supported. If one person consistently takes more than they give, the relationship can become lopsided and unsustainable over time. Setting and respecting boundaries is crucial in any relationship. Being self-aware about how often you seek help ensures that you respect your friends' time and emotional capacity, fostering a healthier and more balanced dynamic. While it's important to have a support system, it's equally important to develop self-reliance. Over-dependence on friends can hinder your personal growth and ability to handle challenges independently. Friends also need to maintain their own positivity and mental health. Continuously focusing on your issues can be draining for them, potentially affecting their ability to stay positive and supportive.

By being mindful of these factors, you can ensure that your friendships remain strong, balanced, and mutually beneficial. This consideration helps create a supportive environment where both parties can thrive, fostering long-lasting and meaningful connections.

We don't always know the purpose of people in our lives, nor do we fully understand our purpose in theirs. While we remain cautious and may keep certain things to ourselves, at this stage in the relationship, we recognize that they are trustworthy. They may not be perfect and can make mistakes, but we know they have our best interests at heart.

- Trustworthy friends have demonstrated reliability and have earned your trust over time. You feel comfortable sharing personal thoughts and experiences with them. They will not judge you, and you are both comfortable with being authentic around each other.
- They offer emotional support during difficult times and celebrate your successes, showing that they genuinely care

about your well-being. They listen to you and want to help you through the process even if they are inconvenienced.

- There is a mutual understanding of open and honest communication. You can discuss sensitive topics without fear of judgment. Both of you understand not all conflict is negative or bad.

- Living Room friends often share common interests or values, which fosters a deeper connection and makes spending time together enjoyable. You have very similar core values that complement each other's life.

- They understand and respect your boundaries, knowing when to give you space and when to engage more deeply. They have a secure attachment type with an occasional anxious or avoidant. If you do, you grace each other in and talk it through, honoring each other's boundaries.

- You can count on them to be there for you when needed, whether it's for a listening ear or practical support. You feel better talking with them, and you can emotionally regulate.

- They create a safe space where you can be yourself without fear of criticism or judgment, allowing for vulnerability. You respect each other's differences and understand we are all unique.

- The friendship is balanced, with both parties contributing to the relationship and supporting each other. Your emotional energy is not drained when you are around them, and you feel uplifted when you spend time together.

- Living Room friends are open to personal growth and are willing to navigate challenges together, strengthening the bond.

You do not feel threatened when the other is spending time with new people or fulfilling dreams.

- Interactions with them feel relaxed and natural, akin to being in a comfortable living room where you can be yourself. They are safe people for you and enjoy that you can be who you are.

In the Living Room, we can express and create boundaries without shame or guilt. We understand each other's strengths and areas for growth, yet we appreciate and love each other for who we are.

Enforcing boundaries in this space is seen as a form of self-respect for both sides of the relationship. If someone oversteps, we feel comfortable addressing it, which helps us maintain our own self-respect and self-care practices.

I have seen this the most often in young adults starting out in life as life circumstances happen—they have children, move away, start careers in new places, and follow different priorities as they grow and change. As much as we want things to stay safe and the same, we need to create our own lives with new friends and priorities. It is common for some of our friends to resist change and the new boundaries we are setting. They will ask why we are not around as much, if we do not want to be friends, and will make us feel shame for moving on with our lives without them.

What a Living Room Friend Looks Like

The transition from the Porch to the Living Room in a friendship is marked by a significant deepening of trust and intimacy. Here are some characteristics of someone who has made this transition:

- They are willing to share personal stories, feelings, and thoughts that they wouldn't disclose to just anyone. This openness is a sign of trust and a belief that their vulnerability will be handled with care.

- They are there for you not just during the good times but also when you're facing challenges. They offer a shoulder to lean on and are willing to help in any way they can.

- There is a strong sense of mutual understanding and empathy. They can often sense how you're feeling and offer support or space as needed without you having to ask.

- While not identical in every way, there is often a significant overlap in core values and beliefs, which forms the basis for deep and meaningful conversations and a sense of camaraderie.

- They are dependable and follow through on their promises. You know you can count on them to be there when they say they will.

- Even though you're close, they respect your boundaries and personal space. They understand that everyone needs time to themselves and that being close doesn't mean being together all the time.

- Time spent together is enjoyable and something you both look forward to. There's a sense of ease and comfort in each other's presence.

- They know your flaws and accept you as you are without trying to change you. This acceptance is reciprocal.

- You have a history of shared experiences that have brought you closer together. These memories serve as a foundation for your relationship.

- They take an active interest in your life, remembering important events and following up on ongoing situations. You do the same for them.

When someone enters the Living Room of your life, it signifies a close, trusted friendship where you can truly be yourself, and there is a strong sense of mutual care and commitment. This is an example of people in the Living Room who share the same core beliefs. However, their personalities may differ—one may be very structured and dislike changes, while the other is more carefree and prefers to go with the flow.

I have a friend who often makes plans when she feels energized, but when the event comes around, she might choose to cancel. Personally, I don't have a problem with this. She knows which events I would prefer her not to cancel and which ones I am more flexible about. This understanding works well for us because I often do the same thing. We respect each other's boundaries and communicate openly about our expectations.

In contrast, I know others who would be very upset if there was a cancellation. If I were in a scenario with such friends, I would make sure that I was 100 percent committed before saying yes, knowing they would not appreciate a last-minute change.

Understanding and respecting each other's boundaries, as long as it does not affect your core values, is crucial in maintaining healthy relationships.

In our Living Room, we don't need perfection from ourselves or from others. What matters is the mutual respect for each other's boundaries and the understanding that we all have different needs and ways of interacting. This respect creates a harmonious environment where everyone feels valued and understood, even if our approaches and priorities differ.

Is Your Friend Ready to Change Rooms?

I am often asked about the appropriate time for a person to be in each room before they change rooms or decide they are here to stay. While there is no specific universal timeline as to how long a person should be in each room in our house—be it the Curb, Porch, Living Room, or Kitchen—every relationship is different in how they connect and the core values and the deep experiences they share.

However, before progressing to the next level in a relationship, I can offer a general rule of a minimum of at least three months. I chose this time because studies show that the three-month mark is when you start to see the real person. People can only mimic for so long before their true personalities and quirks come out. The progression through these spaces is highly individual and depends on numerous factors, including:

- Each person's comfort with intimacy and sharing varies widely.
- Prior relationships and experiences can influence how quickly or slowly someone opens up to new people.
- The level of natural compatibility and shared interests can accelerate or slow down the progression.

- Effective communication can help both parties understand where they stand and when they are ready to move to a deeper level of trust and sharing.
- The rate at which trust is established is crucial and varies greatly between relationships.
- Sometimes, external factors such as life events, stressors, or transitions can affect the pace of a relationship's development.
- The effort and time both individuals invest in the relationship contribute to its growth.
- The emotional state and availability of each person will also play a role in how the relationship develops.

With all that being said, here is a general breakdown. Remember Jamie and Alex in chapter two? Let's see how they navigate changing rooms as trust develops.

Jamie and Alex

The Curb – A Chance Encounter (Month 1) – Jamie and Alex first met at a community book club. They shared a brief conversation about their favorite authors and exchanged smiles. This was the Curb, where they were just two people who happened to be at the same place at the same time.

The Porch – Casual Acquaintance (Months 2–3) – Over the next few meetings, Jamie and Alex found themselves gravitating toward each other during discussions. They began to chat more before and after the book club, discussing not just books but also movies and local events. They decided to connect on social media, liking and commenting on each other's posts. This was the Porch, a place of friendly but still superficial interactions.

Stepping through the Door (Months 4-6)
– One evening, after the book club, they went for a coffee together. Here, the conversation deepened. Jamie shared about her love for painting, and Alex talked about her passion for music. They discovered shared interests and mutual friends. They began to meet for coffee regularly, and their conversations started to include more personal topics, like their families and aspirations.

Milestone: The first time they reached out to each other for advice on a personal matter marked their step through the door from the Porch into the house.

The Living Room – Growing Trust (Months 7–9) –
As the months passed, Jamie and Alex's friendship grew stronger. They were there for each other during stressful times at work, offering support and a listening ear. They celebrated each other's successes and shared quiet moments of disappointment.

Milestone: A key moment was when Jamie confided in Alex about her anxiety issues. Alex responded with empathy, sharing her own struggles with stress. This mutual vulnerability was the cornerstone of their entry into the Living Room.

In general, it is important for the progression through these stages to feel natural and unforced. It's crucial for both parties to feel comfortable and ready to move forward. Some relationships may move through these stages quickly, while others may take months or years to develop. The key is that the progression is mutual and respectful of each person's feelings and boundaries.

Psychologists often emphasize the importance of taking the time to get to know someone and building a foundation of trust before moving into deeper levels of emotional intimacy. This approach tends to facilitate healthier, more sustainable relationships. However, the most important factor is that the pace at which a relationship progresses works for both individuals involved.

Jamie and Alex: The Rest of Their Story

Jamie and Alex's transition from the Porch to the Living Room began one evening when a sudden downpour caught them as they were leaving the book club. They dashed to a nearby café to wait out the storm. As they sipped their coffees, the conversation took a turn from the usual light banter to something more substantial. Jamie mentioned how the rain reminded her of her childhood in the countryside, and for the first time, she opened up about her nostalgic feelings and the sense of loss for a simpler time.

Alex listened intently, sharing a similar sentiment about missing her hometown. This exchange sparked a deeper connection, and they both felt a sense of camaraderie, knowing they shared common ground. Over the next few weeks, their conversations naturally delved into more personal topics. They discussed their dreams, fears, and the challenges they were facing in their current lives.

The defining moment that moved Jamie and Alex from the Porch to the Living Room occurred when Jamie experienced a family emergency. Feeling overwhelmed, Jamie texted Alex, unsure if it was too much to share. Alex responded immediately with genuine concern and offered to help in any way she could. They spent the afternoon together, with Alex providing a comforting presence and helping Jamie navigate the situation.

This act of kindness and support was reciprocated a month later when Alex faced a professional setback. Feeling disheartened, Alex reached out to Jamie, who by then had become a trusted confidant. Jamie offered not only words of encouragement but also helped Alex brainstorm solutions and plan a way forward.

These exchanges marked their entry into the Living Room, a space where they felt comfortable sharing their inner thoughts and relying on each other for support. The mutual trust and willingness to be vulnerable transformed their friendship from a casual acquaintance to a deep and meaningful connection. They started to prioritize their meetups, setting aside time to be there for each other, and their friendship blossomed into one where they could be their true selves without the masks people often wear in more public spaces.

A friend should care about how their actions affect you. If they dismiss your feelings or seem indifferent to your discomfort or pain, it's a sign that the friendship may not be as caring as it should be.

When Your Boundaries Are Pushed in the Living Room

Once we have moved someone to the Living Room, it does not mean they stay there. Something to remember in the Living Room that while we are still connected need to be aware of, for example, a person who oversteps boundaries may also be showing a lack of communication skills or a willingness to listen, both of which are key components of a healthy friendship. We want to be aware of and decide if we want to continually have conversations about communications and boundaries or realize they are Porch friends and act accordingly. Be aware of their intentions, whether they understand what they are doing, and if they should be in the Living Room at all.

I want to add, like the Porch, if you choose you can have several levels in the Living Room as well. I have people I trust, love, and respect who are there for me and will support me to the best of their abilities. Remember: Everybody is doing their best. This is another example of people having different levels of what they consider mentally healthy based on their personal experiences.

Just because someone in your Living Room does not have ill intentions, it doesn't mean their behavior should be dismissed if they continually use your words against you or betray you in some way. In the Living Room or any other room, it's crucial to maintain and protect your boundaries. Sometimes, people may become so comfortable that they try to overstep and push those boundaries.

If someone oversteps boundaries early on, it may indicate differing expectations for the friendship, suggesting you might not be as compatible as you hoped. Early boundary violations can be indicative of future conflicts. If someone doesn't respect small boundaries, they might not respect more significant ones later on.

For example, someone may exhibit behavior that mimics a Living Room friend—they say they are there for you and share personal information. On the surface, it may appear that you are in their Living Room. However, it's essential to remember that everyone has different standards for themselves and their friends. What seems important to you may not hold the same value to them. Just because their behavior suggests a closer relationship doesn't mean it aligns with your perception. They may see you as a Kitchen friend, while you consider them a Porch friend. This is one reason we don't share which room our friends are in.

You need to know what you want from a friend for each room in your house. I pay attention to what I want in a friend in my Living Room. If I feel strongly about a certain standard or issues happening, I may place them in my Living Room. However, if their behavior crosses my core values, I will speak up and possibly move them to the Porch. If someone starts a conversation and asks my opinion, I will give it freely because they are in my Living Room, and they know it comes from a place of love. If you respect each other's beliefs, most friendships will remain intact. Issues arise when we try to impose our beliefs on someone who is not interested in them.

In the concept of emotional spaces within relationships, if someone is in the Living Room, it means they have reached a level of closeness and trust. However, certain boundaries, if crossed, could lead to a person being removed from this space of intimacy.

These boundaries include:

- If a person reveals confidences or betrays the trust that has been built up, this can be a severe violation. This might warrant distancing for a period of time to evaluate if they should stay in the room or move to a different room where you feel safer.

- Consistent disrespect, whether through words or actions, can undermine the foundation of mutual respect that the Living Room level of intimacy requires. If this happens, they need to be moved to a different room. This helps establish an internal boundary, ensuring you don't reveal too much of yourself. When you see them, you know which room they are in and how much transparency is appropriate for that person. Because trust was built, it might feel natural to continue disclosing personal information out of familiarity, even though they have betrayed your trust. Moving them to a different room is not enough; you must remind yourself which room they are now in so that you act according to their behavior.

- Relationships require give-and-take. If one party is always giving while the other is always taking, this imbalance can strain the relationship. For example, if one person is always trauma-dumping without any consideration of the other person's mental health, then the relationship is not reciprocal.

- If an individual repeatedly ignores or disrespects personal boundaries after they have been communicated, this can be a reason to reassess their place in one's emotional space. In my opinion, this is nonnegotiable. If they are not respecting your boundaries, regardless of whether they agree or not, the respect is not there, and they need to move rooms. Boundaries are very important in a relationship. This might sound harsh, but if they don't respect my boundaries, they are at the Curb. I am not rude or disrespectful; they won't even know. However, for my own mental health, I will not share personal information with them—they are not in my Living Room.

- Patterns of manipulation, abuse, gaslighting, or other toxic behaviors necessitate the removal of a person from our close personal space for the sake of our mental and emotional well-being. Just to be clear, this is not acceptable, and they would not be in my life. If, for some reason, they must be in my life, they are at the Curb.

- If someone proves to be unreliable or inconsistent to the point where it negatively affects the other person, it might be necessary to reconsider their closeness in the relationship. These types of friends are Porch friends for me. While I may enjoy their company and they haven't done anything to harm me, this does not mean they are in my Living Room. They will be either at the Curb or on the Porch. Not everyone has ill intentions; sometimes, people simply lack the emotional intelligence to be the type of friend you need. Some may have challenges in their own lives, and just getting up and out of the house could be a struggle.

- If an individual fails to provide support during critical times or is unsupportive of one's goals and aspirations, this can diminish the emotional connection.

It's important to note that while these boundaries are common, they are not exhaustive, and individual relationships may have unique boundaries based on personal values and experiences. Communication about these boundaries is key, and ideally, issues should be addressed before they reach a point where removing someone from the Living Room is considered. If such a situation does arise, it should be handled with care, honesty, and respect for both parties' well-being.

Jordan and Taylor

Let's see what happens in an unhealthy relationship and what overstepping boundaries looks like. To illustrate this, let's meet Jordan and Taylor.

> Jordan had always valued her Sunday family time. Despite knowing this, Taylor would frequently call or

drop by unannounced on Sundays, expecting Jordan to be available. One particular Sunday, Taylor showed up during a family birthday celebration, insisting on joining without an invitation. This disregard for Jordan's boundaries caused tension, signaling a red flag in their friendship.

Whenever Taylor was going through a rough patch, Jordan was there to provide support. However, when Jordan's pet fell ill and she needed someone to talk to, Taylor brushed off the concern, claiming she was too busy. Jordan began to feel like their friendship was a one-way street.

Taylor had a tendency to focus on the negative aspects of life. Each conversation was dominated by complaints and pessimism, leaving Jordan emotionally drained. Despite attempts to steer conversations toward more positive topics, Taylor's persistent negativity began to take a toll on Jordan's outlook on life.

Taylor often used guilt to influence Jordan's decisions. If Jordan made plans with other friends, Taylor would sulk and remind her of a past favor, suggesting that Jordan owed her the time. This manipulative tactic left Jordan feeling trapped and resentful.

Jordan had confided in Taylor about a sensitive family matter, asking her to keep it private. To Jordan's dismay, she later discovered that Taylor had shared this information with mutual friends under the guise of "concern," violating Jordan's trust and privacy.

Taylor disliked Jordan's growing friendship with a new colleague. She made snide remarks about the colleague and questioned Jordan's loyalty. Taylor's jealousy manifested in possessive behavior, trying to monopolize Jordan's time and undermining other friendships.

After a misunderstanding, Jordan reached out to Taylor to clear the air. Instead of apologizing or discussing the issue, Taylor became defensive and dismissed Jordan's feelings. This unwillingness to resolve conflicts put a strain on their friendship.

Jordan learned not to count on Taylor's word. Taylor would often cancel plans at the last minute or forget commitments altogether. Jordan felt disappointed and undervalued, realizing that Taylor's unreliability was a pattern, not an exception.

When Jordan expressed hurt over Taylor's actions, Taylor's response was indifferent. She seemed more concerned with justifying her behavior than acknowledging Jordan's feelings. This disregard was the final red flag that made Jordan question the health of their friendship.

In the end, Jordan understood that the Living Room of her emotional house needed to be a place of mutual respect and support. It was a difficult decision, but Jordan decided to have an honest conversation with Taylor about these red flags and the need for change. Whether their friendship could weather this storm and evolve into a healthier dynamic remained to be seen, but Jordan knew that acknowledging these issues was the first step toward either healing the friendship or setting the boundaries necessary for her own emotional well-being.

Jordan's decision to address the issues head-on was a crucial step in reclaiming their sense of peace and respect in their relationships. It underscored the importance of clear boundaries and mutual respect in any friendship. Whether Taylor would be willing to change and respect these boundaries was uncertain, but Jordan was prepared to prioritize her own emotional health, even if it meant distancing herself from a toxic relationship and moving Taylor to the Porch where she would not share vulnerable information.

Determining whether to rebuild trust hinges on the friendship's depth and the impact of the betrayal. You must ask yourself whether the relationship holds enough significance to warrant the effort of repair. Weigh the history of mutual support against the severity of the trust breach.

Only you will know the answer to this; however, if repairing is the chosen route, open communication becomes critical. Engage in a dialogue about the betrayal, expressing feelings without assigning blame. It's about taking responsibility and showing genuine remorse. Reestablishing trust may involve setting new boundaries, with actions aligned to promises made, signifying a commitment to change.

Alternatively, if the decision is to let go, the focus should shift to healing. This involves acknowledging pain without letting it define your self-worth. Engaging in self-care practices, such as meditation or journaling, can aid the healing process. Embrace the experience as a part of growth, learning to invest trust in relationships cautiously moving forward.

To safeguard against the sting of betrayal by a close friend, pro-actively set standards for interpersonal relationships. This involves being selective with friendships, promoting transparency in communication, and clearly defining trust parameters.

When selecting friends, consider the potential friend's history with others, their values, and consistency in behavior. Remember in Chapter One, we discussed Bob's wife, Karen, and how she was sharing information about Bob's co-workers? This would be the type of action in others we want to be aware of. While they wouldn't have these before being moved to your Living Room, they could develop them over time. Perhaps they have an individual in their life who is negative and changing the dynamic of their personality, thereby changing the dynamics of your relationship with them. It's advisable to:

- Observe how the individual treats people in various scenarios.
- Align with those whose principles mirror your own.

The Living Room of your emotional house is there to build stronger connections with friends who help you in life, encourage you, and support your goals and dreams. It's a space for those with whom you have a history of mutual respect. Moving people too quickly to the Living Room can be risky; if they betray your trust, they may end up not just back on the Porch but either at the Curb or out of your life entirely. When people are in our Living Room, an act of betrayal runs deeper. We are offended by their actions because we trusted them and believed in the closeness of the relationship.

We need to hold people accountable for their actions if they are mentally capable of it. If we move them too soon, we will not be able to evaluate whether they are worthy of being a Living Room friend.

This is not to say they are not worthy people, but rather to question whether we are emotionally available to be the kind of friend others would like.

There was a time in my life when I did not see the value in friends. My mother did not have people who came over; she did not go out with others, so I had no reference and honestly couldn't understand why other people needed the connection. I can recall when our kids were in school, I did have other mom friends who would ask to go to the grocery store together, and that was so confusing for me. Why would I want to spend more time out of my day going to the store with someone else? In that instance, I was not ready to be a Living Room friend; I was more of a Porch friend for sure.

Understanding the different levels of friendship and the appropriate boundaries for each can help protect your emotional well-being. Not everyone is meant to be in your Living Room, and that's okay. Some people are better suited to be Porch friends or even acquaintances. By being mindful of who you allow into your inner circle, you can build stronger, more supportive relationships that enrich your life.

Ultimately, the key is to be intentional about your friendships, recognizing that they require effort, trust, and mutual respect. Whether you choose to repair a friendship or let it go, the most important thing is to ensure that your relational house remains a sanctuary of peace, support, and genuine connection.

The Living Room is a complicated space, one where we want to let our guard down and not have to worry. However, it's important to remain aware of our actions, mindset, and mental health. Some people will move in and out of this room, but if we find ourselves moving them too often, we should consider whether they are truly Porch friends.

Only you can determine where people in your life should be. Trust your instincts and remember that your mental health and what you seek in relationships are paramount.

Questioning Trust: Who Really Belongs in Your Living Room?

CHAPTER 5

The Kitchen

Welcome to the Kitchen! This is the most trusted and sacred of all the rooms, where only a select few are invited. Think of it as a secret society for those who truly know you, like you have your own unspoken code. A glance is all it takes to understand each other in this room. It was when my husband, Wally, and I got married and began building a life together with our kids that I began to understand the importance of the Kitchen. This is where I feel safe and protected; I know that whoever is in this room will have my back, and I know I can count on them for unconditional love and support. Personally, I have the fewest people in this room.

In previous chapters, I mentioned my journey in learning about friendship boundaries. Initially, I realized I was an open book with everyone I knew in my Kitchen. Over time, I came to understand that this space is reserved for those who have proven to be safe and trustworthy.

Here, we gather to share deep discussions and offer unconditional support, fostering personal growth and helping each other achieve our goals and dreams. This is the space where we can be as vulnerable as we need to be.

These circles are often very small, typically including significant others, children, close friends, and parents. If you are fortunate enough to have friends in your Kitchen, cherish and cultivate these special relationships. To be honest, it doesn't happen very often. Enjoy it while it is there, as times and circumstances can change a relationship.

While I have labeled these rooms in a way that resonates with me, remember this is your house, and you can label them differently if you wish. I favor the Kitchen because it's where my husband and kids hang out, where we talk and share our day—the good, the bad, and the ugly.

We laugh here, we cry, and we share personal stories.

If I can get my family together in one room to share, it would be the Kitchen. And if we end up watching a movie afterward, this mom's heart is full and happy! Just saying, in case my kids are reading this— call your mother.

Be Watchful, Even in the Kitchen

Over the years, I have experienced the heartbreak of sharing too much with the wrong person. After many such experiences, I went to therapy to understand this behavior and learn to manage my feelings, seeking to understand why I often felt overwhelmed. Boundaries are crucial—they're not easy to set, but they are necessary. We work hard at protecting our inner peace, our ability to be the best version of ourselves, and our desire to serve our purpose. This is the room where we will receive the most support and, honestly, the most heartbreak.

It always hurts the most when we are betrayed by the ones we trusted the most. This is why we need to ensure that whoever is in this room is someone we fully trust. Sometimes, betrayal happens unintentionally, and this will determine where in the house they should be for a while until a trusted relationship is rebuilt.

Be careful in this room. I have seen many times that we don't pay attention to the red flags that come up. As I mentioned before, circumstances can change the way people react. When you over-idealize someone, you set yourself up for disappointment when they inevitably fail to meet those unrealistic expectations. We tend to get comfortable with people in this room because we have known them the longest and trust them without question. However, we are all human and can falter. Be aware of potential problems that could arise with the people in your Kitchen. You might misjudge situations or overlook important red flags because you are too focused on their perceived perfection. We think the people in this room would never harm us, and while they may not consciously realize it, either we or others will disappoint us at some point.

In the Kitchen and Living Room, boundaries are just as important, and you must be comfortable with those in these rooms. It's a space to be close with friends and family but also a place to respect each other's limits and avoid overwhelming one another. Friendships thrive here, built on understanding and balance, where you can relax together without feeling like too much of a burden.

But here's the beauty: If you have that one best friend—the one you talk to every day, where boundaries are comfortably blurred yet respected, and both of you feel perfectly aligned—that's something truly special. Not every friendship works this way, but when you find someone with whom your needs and rhythms naturally sync, cherish it. *Side note: If you're one of the lucky ones with a friend like this, where you don't feel like you have to hold back, then embrace it fully! A friend who aligns with you, respects you, and shares in the blurred healthy, respectful boundaries of closeness—that's a blessing.*

Good friendships come in many forms, but the best ones, the ones that feel like the living room and Kitchen of our lives, are those that let us be ourselves, safe in the comfort of mutual understanding.

It's important to remember that over-idealization can foster unhealthy dependency, where you rely too much on these individuals for your emotional or psychological well-being, causing you to lose your autonomy and independence, which are both necessary for personal growth and living your purpose. It can prevent both you and the other person from growing, as you might avoid addressing real issues or challenges in the relationship.

When I first started therapy, most people were in my Kitchen, with only those exhibiting truly bad behavior moved to the Curb. In other words, I perceived you as either very close or not someone I wanted to associate with at all. Some of that was due to a lack of maturity, but most of it stemmed from an inability to create boundaries. I struggled to determine who I could trust with certain information and even lost my sense of self because I was too busy trying to manage other people's emotions and behaviors.

If you find yourself in this position, here are some signs that you are losing yourself in your relationships:

- You no longer do the things you once enjoyed. You are constantly making sacrifices or compromising your own needs.

- You might be seeing these people through "rose-colored glasses," attributing qualities and virtues to them that they may not actually possess.

- You could be minimizing or ignoring their flaws, mistakes, or negative behaviors because you hold them in such high esteem. You may disregard your personal boundaries to please the people in this room.

- This idealization can lead to an imbalanced view of the relationship, where you see it as perfect or without issues, which is seldom the case in reality. You might feel the need to consult with the people in this room for everything and spend less time with friends or family you were once close to.

Realistic views of the people in your Kitchen lead to healthier, more balanced relationships. It allows for genuine connections based on mutual understanding and acceptance of each other's strengths and weaknesses. Recognizing that everyone has flaws and limitations helps you grow and develop more resilient, adaptable relationships. Being in touch with reality and accepting the possibility of betrayal enables you to address conflicts and issues effectively rather than sweeping them under the rug due to idealization. This approach allows us to create boundaries in a healthy way, keeping the relationship strong with the comfort that they are still in our Kitchen. Remember, healthy relationships involve protecting your boundaries and allowing others to maintain theirs as well. Real support comes from understanding and accepting each other as you are, not as idealized versions of yourselves.

To maintain a healthy relationship in the Kitchen that fosters independence and growth, regularly reflect on your relationships and be honest about each person's strengths and weaknesses. Embrace open and honest communication where both parties feel safe to express their true selves, including their flaws and struggles. Be realistic about what the relationship is and is not, understanding that no one is perfect and that everyone has their unique set of challenges and strengths.

Once I mentally placed people in different rooms, I could appreciate them as individuals. I knew who they were and no longer needed to guess or feel ashamed for trusting others.

Faux Kitchen Behaviors

Mimicking is something people do for several reasons, and this applies to all Rooms in Your House. I include it in this chapter because, by now, you understand the relationships you are fostering and can gain perspective on mimics and relationships built on trust. It's important to recognize that people can mimic different behaviors to gain your trust. This was a significant lesson for me; I often based what I would share on the moment rather than on their past behavior. I was trusting everyone based on the moment, and we know that in moments, people can act as if they are trustworthy.

Here are some examples of how others can mimic to gain trust:

- Verbal Mimicking: Adopting similar speech patterns, tone of voice, or vocabulary.
- Non-Verbal Mimicking: Mirroring body language, gestures, or facial expressions.
- Emotional Mimicking: Matching your emotions or reactions, such as your enthusiasm, empathy, or excitement. Be cautious of someone who quickly adopts the same emotional state as you; if it feels forced or insincere, be wary.

Some red flags I've noticed over the years include inconsistent behaviors—people who say one thing to you and something different to their significant other or another close friend. In other words, their words and actions don't match, indicating a lack of authenticity. Another red flag is a lack of individuality; they mimic you without expressing their own thoughts, opinions, or preferences. Mutual respect is essential for healthy relationships. Trust your gut and listen to your instincts. You may not always notice the mimicking, but I assure you, from experience, your gut will know.

Further examples include mimicking what a Kitchen or Living Room friend would look like:

> The Mimic: They listen attentively, nodding and responding appropriately to make you feel heard. Reality Check: Notice if they remember and act on what you've shared

over time or if their listening is superficial and doesn't lead to meaningful action.

The Mimic: They frequently offer to help with tasks or problems. Reality Check: Evaluate if their offers of help are followed through and if they're willing to assist without expecting something in return.

The Mimic: They share personal stories or vulnerabilities to create a sense of mutual trust. Reality Check: Consider if their sharing is reciprocal and genuine or if it feels calculated to gain your trust.

The Mimic: They show empathy and understanding when you share your problems. Reality Check: Observe if their empathy translates into consistent, supportive actions or if it's just words without follow-through.

The Mimic: They use humor, shared interests, and common values to build a sense of rapport. Reality Check: Assess if the rapport is deep and meaningful or if it feels like they're mirroring your interests to gain favor.

Mimicking can occur on different levels and is not necessarily bad; we mimic—or in healthy relationships, it's called *mirroring*—in order to build healthy relationships when we want to establish a connection. We do this in personal relationships, when just meeting someone, in work situations when starting a new job, and salespeople use this all the time. Healthcare professionals also mimic behavior to establish trust. For example, if you are sitting with your legs crossed, the other person may do this as well to establish a connection. If I am mimicking your behavior, you may feel we are connected. However, we need to be aware of what mimicking is and how to look for the signs if we want to ensure the rooms in our house are filled with the right people.

This awareness helped me early on when I found myself in vulnerable situations. I could gather myself, assess where they stood in terms of trust, and create an action plan. For example, if someone is mimicking and trying to establish a connection, and I know they are on the Curb or Porch, I work on stopping myself from being too vulnerable and open with my personal life or sharing too much information too quickly.

If someone was on my Curb, working really hard to mimic, telling me what I want to hear, expressing the same core values as me, agreeing with everything i say, and having no original thoughts or beliefs, they would stay on my Curb.

How we determine the level of mimicking and if it will affect the relationship depends on the intent and extent of the behavior. Let's go over some of the potential negative impacts people who mimic can have on healthy relationships.

The inauthenticity of a relationship, for example, where an individual is mimicking excessively or manipulatively, can lead to inauthentic interactions. Any relationships built on false pretenses or exaggerated similarities may lack genuine connection and trust. A house of cards, per se, appears strong, but with the first wind, the house will go down.

When someone mimics as a tool for manipulation, it can undermine trust and lead to feelings of betrayal once the true intentions are revealed. Initially, we may perceive this behavior positively because these individuals seem similar to ourselves. However, this can cause significant harm to the relationship, as the foundation of trust is compromised.

If we are not aware of people who mimic to build trust, we become over-reliant on the actual behavior, which can result in the loss of one's individuality and authenticity. We become desensitized to what is authentic or not, and we may start mimicking ourselves, losing our individuality. This can lead to an imbalance in the relationship, where one person feels they are not truly known or valued for who they are. In other words, there are no real connections, and no real bonding occurs. Relationships heavily based on mimicry may remain superficial and lack depth. Without genuine understanding and acceptance, the relationship might not withstand challenges and deeper emotional needs. We may eventually lose our sense of self because we are unable to distinguish between authentic interactions and mimicked behavior. This can happen at work as well; we believe we are connected with our coworkers, but once they leave, we never hear from them again. There was a perceived connection, but it now seems they were merely mimicking.

This lack of genuine connection can be particularly evident in professional settings. We might believe we have a rapport with our coworkers, but once they leave the job, the relationship often fades, revealing that the connection was superficial. They were mimicking behaviors to fit in or to gain our trust temporarily rather than building a lasting, authentic relationship.

In the years before I understood the spaces in my own house, I fell victim to those who would mimic, those who used my own words against me. Each time, I would connect with them, forgetting past betrayals, drawn in by what I wanted to see in a friend. They mirrored the behaviors of a best friend, just enough to let me feel safe, to let me believe I could trust them. I'd open up, sharing pieces of myself, becoming vulnerable. And that was always when they'd reveal themselves, slipping back into who they truly were—the ones who should have stayed on the Porch or perhaps on the Curb.

This pattern repeated, time and again, until I finally prepared myself each time I saw them. I learned to keep a map of the rooms in my mind, to know exactly where they belonged within the walls of my house. I became cautious, no longer falling prey to the behavior that once made me so open.

To safeguard against these potential negative impacts, it's crucial to stay attuned to both your instincts and the consistency of others' behaviors. Trust should be built on genuine interactions and mutual respect, not solely on surface-level similarities. By remaining mindful of these dynamics, you can foster relationships that are both authentic and resilient. You want people who are capable of withstanding the tests of time and adversity, for those in your Living Room and Kitchen, of course. The Porch friends are fun, and we love hanging out with them, but we do not share personal information.

- Not all situations of mimicking are negative; in fact, it can help establish initial connections and ease social interactions. In the early stages of a relationship, mimicking or mirroring behaviors and sharing some likes and dislikes can facilitate trust and rapport, making people feel more comfortable and understood.

- When used naturally and with good intentions, mimicry/ mirroring can demonstrate empathy and enhance mutual understanding. This can strengthen the emotional bond and improve communication within the relationship. It helps us break down the walls of trust for a bit, allowing the other person in without shutting them out. It builds enough of a connection to open our hearts to new relationships. However, never forget which room they are in your house; mimics are good and will try to establish connectedness sooner than is healthy.

- In most social situations, we have a subculture of written and unwritten social norms. People who mimic the group's behaviors can help themselves adapt to new cultural or social environments, fostering inclusivity and acceptance. It can bridge gaps between different backgrounds, promoting harmony and cooperation.

- In healthy relationships, it is important to be self-aware of your own behaviors and motivations for mimicking. Ensure it stems from a genuine place of empathy and connection rather than manipulation. Be authentic and strive to balance mimicking with authenticity when building rapport. Don't go against your core values to belong to a group; if you have to compromise your beliefs, they are not your people, and you will come across as someone they cannot trust, someone who is not authentic. Share your true thoughts, feelings, and personality to build a deeper, more genuine connection. Respect each other's individuality. Celebrate differences as well as similarities and ensure that both parties feel valued for who they truly are.

While mimicry can play a role in building initial connections and fostering empathy, it's crucial to maintain authenticity and self-awareness to ensure that relationships are built on genuine trust and understanding. By balancing mimicry with honest communication and mutual respect, you can create deeper, more meaningful connections.

Who Should Be in This Kitchen of Ours?

This is my list of people in my Kitchen, and I feel this is who should be your closest circle. This is your house and your rules. Be cautious, as the point of this book is to hold your boundaries and ensure you are not sharing information with those who cannot appreciate you for who you are and will not divulge your secrets, dreams, and goals.

Significant Others: These are our partners in life who share our goals and dreams. They offer support and companionship. However, if you find yourself in a relationship where your partner is being abusive, whether emotionally or physically, it may be necessary to reconsider their place in your Kitchen. In such situations, seeking professional help is crucial. It has been my experience that overcoming these challenges alone can be incredibly difficult. Those who engage in mental abuse often have a history of manipulating others to feel at fault, making it even more important to seek external support.

Close Family Members: Parents, siblings, or children who offer un-wavering support and love belong in the Kitchen. However, not all family members provide the trust and support required for this intimate space. This doesn't mean they should be removed from your life entirely. For instance, I have a friend whose brother, despite being loved dearly, doesn't always tell the truth. For his own personal reasons, this is his issue, not hers. To maintain a supportive yet safe relationship with him, she has decided that her brother belongs in the Living Room. He hasn't betrayed her, but she cannot trust him with all aspects of her life. This is a safe place where she knows how much to share with him.

Best Friends: These are friends who have proven their loyalty and trustworthiness over time. They have shared experiences with you and have never betrayed your confidence. There are some things that are never shared outside this circle.

Mentors or Trusted Advisors: Individuals who provide guidance and support without judgment also play a crucial role. For example, I have a counselor with whom I share many things. They are trusted and non-judgmental, but because we are not friends outside of the office, they would not be in my Kitchen.

Additional Considerations

Acquaintances and Colleagues: While they might play important roles in your life, they generally belong in the outer rooms of your emotional house. These are people you interact with regularly but do not share your deepest thoughts and feelings with. Trust is built over time, and it's important to gauge their intentions and reliability before inviting them into more intimate spaces of your life.

Maintaining Boundaries in the Kitchen

It is essential to maintain clear boundaries to protect your emotional well-being and ensure that your inner circle consists of people who genuinely support and understand you. Here are some tips:

- Regularly evaluate the trustworthiness and reliability of those in your inner circle. Trust is a two-way street and should be nurtured and maintained.
- Foster open and honest communication with those in your Kitchen. Misunderstandings can be avoided when everyone feels comfortable expressing their thoughts and feelings.
- Celebrate the differences as well as the similarities. Ensure that both parties feel valued for who they truly are.
- Don't hesitate to seek professional guidance when dealing with complex relationships or emotional challenges. Therapists, counselors, and mentors can provide valuable insights and support.

Building and maintaining a supportive inner circle is crucial for personal growth and emotional well-being. By carefully choosing who belongs in your Kitchen and maintaining clear boundaries, you can create a nurturing environment that fosters genuine trust, understanding, and mutual respect. Remember, your house, your rules. Choose wisely and protect your emotional sanctuary.

The Essence of the Kitchen

The Kitchen is a place of deep connection and mutual growth. It's where you can be your true self without fear of judgment, knowing that the people there will support you through thick and thin.

Maintaining this sacred space requires ongoing effort, respect, and a commitment to nurturing these invaluable relationships.

What a Kitchen Friend Looks Like

First, they need to spend time in the other rooms. People in this room usually don't get here quickly; it often takes years to develop this type of relationship. Here are the key elements that help someone earn a place in your Kitchen: They consistently demonstrate reliability and honesty over time. Valuing each other's thoughts, feelings, and boundaries is crucial, as well as offering and giving empathy, understanding, and encouragement. They are genuine and transparent in actions and words, of course, aligning core beliefs and aspirations. Actions and words must match over time, with no hidden agenda with a willingness to share and listen without judgment. It's important to be comfortable, show your true self, and support others in doing the same. This is not a room for your co-workers, casual friends, or family members who show inappropriate behavior.

Once a person has entered the Kitchen, it's important to maintain a strong, mutually respectful relationship by:

- Always be truthful and dependable in your interactions. Trust is the foundation of any close relationship, and maintaining it requires consistent honesty.
- Respect each other's boundaries and personal needs. This includes understanding when someone needs space or time alone and not taking it personally.

- Be there for each other not just emotionally but also in practical ways. Whether it's helping out with tasks or providing a listening ear, showing support in various forms strengthens the bond.

- Ensure that lines of communication are always open. Misunderstandings can be minimized when both parties feel comfortable expressing their thoughts and feelings openly.

- Handling disagreements with maturity and understanding: Disagreements are inevitable, but handling them maturely and with empathy can prevent them from damaging the relationship. Focus on understanding each other's perspectives and finding common ground.

- Create and cherish shared experiences. These memories form the backbone of your relationship and provide a source of joy and connection.

- Support each other's growth and personal development. Celebrate achievements and provide encouragement during challenges. This mutual support helps both individuals thrive.

- Continuously strive to grow and live your purpose. Relationships can stagnate if both parties become complacent. Keep challenging each other to be the best versions of yourselves.

- When people in your Kitchen call you out on your behavior, lack of growth, or poor boundaries, understand that it comes from a place of love. Constructive criticism is essential for personal and relational growth.

- Ensure that the relationship is balanced and that both parties are equally invested. A one-sided relationship can lead to resentment and imbalance. Both individuals should feel valued and supported.

By following these principles, you can maintain strong, healthy, and mutually respectful relationships with those in your Kitchen. These relationships will not only enrich your life but also provide a solid foundation of support and love.

Angela

Angela is a friend of Brenda, a woman I was coaching; they met on their children's first day of kindergarten. Initially, their interactions were casual and focused on their kids, but over time, they discovered they had much more in common. Both loved hiking, had a passion for cooking, and shared similar values about family and personal growth.

Angela consistently showed up for their scheduled class volunteer times, and her reliability extended beyond volunteering at the school. When my client had a family emergency and couldn't attend a critical field trip, Angela took her spot and spent extra hours helping the classroom. Her actions demonstrated that she could be counted on, even in stressful situations.

They respected each other's opinions and boundaries. When they had differing views on certain topics, the discussions were always respectful and enlightening. Angela never tried to impose her beliefs on my client; instead, she listened and valued her perspective.

During the kids' second-grade year, Brenda went through a tough breakup. Angela was there for her, offering a shoulder to cry on and words of encouragement. She didn't just offer platitudes; she actively listened and helped her navigate her emotions. Her empathy and understanding were invaluable.

Angela was always genuine. She didn't pretend to be someone she wasn't, and her honesty was refreshing. Whether she was sharing her struggles with balancing parenting responsibilities, work, or her excitement about a new recipe she tried, she was always her true self.

Shared values and aspirations: They both valued personal growth and had similar aspirations. They would often discuss their future goals, from career ambitions to personal development. This alignment created a strong foundation for their relationship.

Over the years, Angela's actions and words consistently matched. She never had hidden agendas, and her reliability was unwavering. Whether it was small promises or significant commitments, she always followed through.

Open communication: Their communication was always open and honest. They were able to talk about anything, from fears and insecurities to hopes and dreams. This transparency strengthened their bond and built a deep level of trust.

They were comfortable being vulnerable with each other. Brenda was able to share her deepest fears and insecurities, and Angela did the same. This mutual vulnerability created a safe space where they could be their true selves without fear of judgment.

Through these qualities and actions, Angela earned her place in the Kitchen—woohoo for Angela!! She is a trusted friend, and we are happy Brenda has someone she can rely on and be in her corner, as this is a space reserved for the most trusted and valued relationships. Their bond grew stronger over the years, built on a foundation of trust, respect, empathy, and shared values. Angela's consistent reliability, open communication, and genuine nature made her an indispensable part of my client's life. This relationship exemplifies what it means to have someone in your Kitchen: a person who supports you unconditionally, listens without judgment, and helps you grow into the best version of yourself.

This is not to say that either person is perfect; we all have bad days and may say something that would hurt the other. It's the history they have, the times this happens, and the willingness to course-correct the behavior that determines a Kitchen friend.

When Betrayal Happens in the Kitchen: Anne & Karen

Let's meet Karen and Anne. Betrayal in the Kitchen often involves a breach of trust, such as sharing confidential information, failing to provide support during critical times, or acting in self-interest at the expense of the relationship. These actions can cause significant emotional pain and lead to a reevaluation of the relationship's place in one's life.

In the small town—side note, I love small towns, and since I'm writing this book, I'll make my two friends live in one—there lived two friends, Karen and Anne. Their friendship began in junior year of high school, bound together by a shared love for literature. They spent countless hours discussing their favorite books and authors, and over time, Anne became one of Karen's closest confidants. Karen trusted Anne with her deepest thoughts and feelings, believing that Anne would always have her back.

Anne was always reliable. She kept Karen's secrets, showed up when she said she would, and was someone Karen could depend on. During a particularly challenging time when Karen's parents were going through a difficult divorce, Anne was there every step of the way, offering a listening ear and comforting words (trustworthiness).

Their friendship was built on mutual respect. They valued each other's opinions and never tried to change one another. Even when they had different views on certain topics, their discussions were always respectful and enriching (mutual respect).

Anne was incredibly supportive. She celebrated Karen's successes and comforted her during her failures. When Karen struggled with self-doubt, Anne was the one who reminded her of her strengths and encouraged her to keep going (emotional support).

Anne was genuine and honest. She never pretended to be someone she wasn't, and her authenticity made it easy for Karen to be herself around her. They shared their dreams, fears, and everything in between (authenticity).

They had similar values and aspirations. Both wanted to make a positive impact on the world and often discussed their future plans and how they could achieve them together (shared values and goals). They were not envious of each other when the other was achieving more or growing in maturity.

Anne's actions and words were always in sync. She was dependable and never let Karen down. Whether it was a small promise or a significant commitment, she always followed through (consistent behavior).

Their communication was open and honest. They could talk about anything without fear of judgment. This transparency strengthened their bond and built a deep level of trust (open communication).

They were comfortable being vulnerable with each other. Karen shared her deepest fears and insecurities, and Anne did the same. This mutual vulnerability created a safe space where they could be their true selves (vulnerability).

One day, Karen confided in Anne about a deeply personal issue she was facing. It was something she hadn't shared with anyone else, and she trusted Anne completely. A few weeks later, Karen discovered from another friend that Anne had shared her secret with others. Not only had Anne broken Karen's trust, but she had also added her own interpretations, making the situation seem worse than it was (betrayal).

This betrayal cut deeply. Karen felt hurt and confused. She confronted Anne, seeking an explanation. Anne apologized, claiming she hadn't meant any harm and thought she was helping by discussing it with others. However, the damage was done. Karen was unable to objectively look at the situation; she knew Anne's heart and because this had never happened before, she could no longer see Anne in the same light.

Their relationship changed fundamentally for Karen, as she had been hurt in the past and felt the pain over again. The trust that had taken years to build was changed in an instant. Karen found it difficult to confide in Anne again, and their once open and honest communication became strained and awkward. The mutual respect and emotional support that had been the foundation of their friendship were now overshadowed by doubt and mistrust.

Because this was a one-time incident, Karen learned a valuable lesson from this experience: even the closest friendships can falter if trust is broken. She became more cautious about who she confided in, understanding that true friendship requires not just shared interests and values but also unwavering trust and integrity.

Moving Anne to the Porch

Initial Shock and Hurt: The betrayal hit Karen hard. She felt a mix of anger, sadness, and disbelief. Anne had been someone she trusted implicitly, and her actions felt like a deep wound. Karen confronted Anne about it, hoping for an explanation or at least an apology. Anne did apologize, but her reasoning seemed weak and insincere. She claimed she thought it would help if others knew, but Karen couldn't shake the feeling that Anne had done it for gossip rather than support.

Reevaluating the relationship: Karen took some time to reevaluate their relationship. Trust was the cornerstone of their friendship, and without it, everything else felt shaky. She realized that while Anne had been a great friend in many ways, this betrayal was significant enough to change the dynamics of their relationship.

Setting boundaries: Karen was deeply hurt by the situation and decided to move Anne from the Kitchen to the Porch. You may think of this and believe moving to the Living Room would be okay for you, or not moving them at all. That's the nice thing about creating your rooms—they are for you and your boundaries. This meant redefining their friendship and setting new boundaries. While Karen still valued some aspects of their relationship, she could no longer share her deepest thoughts and feelings with Anne. Their interactions became more casual and less intimate.

Communicating the change: Karen had a heartfelt conversation with Anne, explaining how her actions had affected her and why she needed to set new boundaries. She needed time to process her emotions, so she told Anne that while she still cared about her, she needed to protect herself and her trust. Anne seemed to understand, though it was clear she was hurt by the change.

Life on the Porch

Casual Interactions: Their interactions became more surface-level. They still hung out in group settings and enjoyed shared activities, but the deep, heart-to-heart conversations would not be a part of their relationship. They would catch up on general life events, but the intimacy that once defined their friendship was noticeably absent for a while until they could build trust up again.

Maintaining respect: Despite the betrayal, Karen chose to maintain respect and civility. She didn't speak poorly of Anne to others and made an effort to keep their interactions positive. This approach helped her preserve her peace of mind and avoid unnecessary drama.

Learning from the experience: The experience taught Karen valuable lessons about trust and boundaries. She was always cautious about sharing too much information, but this experience helped her see that even Kitchen friends need to have boundaries.

Growth and reflection: Karen spent time reflecting on what had happened and how she could grow from the experience. She realized that while trust can be broken, it also offers an opportunity for personal growth and resilience. She learned to listen to her instincts and to value the people who truly respected and supported her.

Reevaluating the past: Occasionally, Karen would think back to the times when she and Anne were close. While there was a sense of loss, there was also a sense of clarity. She understood that people change and relationships evolve, and sometimes, moving someone to the Porch is necessary for personal well-being.

Rebuilding trust: Over time, Karen and Anne had occasional conversations about what had happened. Anne expressed genuine remorse and made efforts to rebuild trust, though it was a slow and cautious process. While their friendship never returned to its original depth, they managed to find a new balance that worked for both of them.

Life on the Porch was different, but it was also a necessary step in Karen's journey. It allowed her to protect her emotional well-being while still maintaining a cordial relationship with Anne. The experience reinforced the importance of trust and taught Karen to value the people who truly respected and supported her. It was a lesson in resilience, personal growth, and the importance of setting healthy boundaries. Karen emerged stronger and more self-aware, ready to nurture relationships that truly honored the trust and respect she valued so deeply.

It's Okay if Some Family Members Are Not in Your Kitchen

I previously wrote about this, and I want to spend some time here talking about why it's okay if some family members are not in your Kitchen. Others might try to convince you that we need to put family first in all circumstances. While I believe in supporting family members, I do not condone being associated with those who have abused or harmed you in any way. It's important to acknowledge that not all family members should be in your Kitchen simply by virtue of being family. This space is reserved for those who truly support, respect, and uplift you. Here's why some family members might not belong in the Kitchen and why you should not feel guilt, shame, or judgment for keeping your boundaries:

- Some family members may not consistently demonstrate the trustworthiness and reliability required to be in the Kitchen. If their actions and words don't align, or if they have a history of breaking promises, it's essential to recognize that they may not be suitable for this intimate space.

- Family members who do not respect your boundaries—whether emotional, physical, or mental—can create an unsafe environment. It's crucial to maintain boundaries to protect your well-being, even if it means keeping certain family members at a distance.

- If a family member exhibits toxic behavior, such as manipulation, constant criticism, or emotional abuse, they should not be in the Kitchen. Allowing such behavior can harm your mental and emotional health.

- Family members who do not share your core values and goals may not provide the support and understanding you need. It's okay to recognize that while you may love them, they might not align with your vision for personal growth and happiness.

Maintaining these boundaries is not about rejecting family but about protecting your emotional and mental health. It's about ensuring that your Kitchen remains a safe, supportive space where you can thrive. It's perfectly acceptable to prioritize your well-being and surround yourself with those who genuinely care for and respect you.

Protecting Yourself Without Guilt or Shame

Never under any circumstances should you feel guilt or shame for protecting yourself. If other family members will not help you protect yourself, then they don't get an opinion on how you protect yourself.

Maintaining boundaries is an act of self-preservation. It's about protecting your mental and emotional health, which is vital for your overall well-being. The Kitchen is a space for healthy, supportive relationships. Allowing someone who doesn't meet these criteria can disrupt the harmony and safety of this space.

Surrounding yourself with people who respect and support you is essential for personal growth. It's okay to prioritize relationships that foster your development and happiness. You are not obligated to include someone in your Kitchen just because they are family. Relationships should be based on mutual respect, trust, and support, not on obligation or guilt.

It is perfectly acceptable to set boundaries with family members who do not support or respect you. Your Kitchen should be a space reserved for those who contribute positively to your life. By maintaining these boundaries, you protect your well-being and ensure that your relationships are healthy and supportive. Remember, you have the right to prioritize your mental and emotional health, and you should never feel guilty for doing so.

Handling Pushback on Your Boundaries

Let's face it—when we set boundaries, pushback is likely to happen. If it weren't, we wouldn't have needed the boundary in the first place. Some people will press you to the point of second-guessing yourself. They may try to use guilt or shame to make you back down, reacting to the changes you're making because they've lost control. They may even blame you for the shift. But remember, it was *their behavior* that led you to establish this boundary. Stand firm in your decision, knowing that protecting your space is not only valid but necessary. It's perfectly okay to keep your boundaries firm, even when faced with pushback from family or others.

Here's how to handle it:

- When communicating your boundaries, be clear and assertive. Explain why they are important to you and how they help maintain your well-being.

- Be aware that not everyone will understand your boundaries, and it is not your responsibility to ensure they buy into your perspective. In other words, don't try to convince someone else of what you believe in. Some people will never get it, and that is why they should not be in your Kitchen.

Maintaining these boundaries is about protecting your space and ensuring that it remains a place of support and positivity. By doing so, you are prioritizing your mental and emotional health, which is essential for living a fulfilling and balanced life.

Stand firm in your boundaries even if others push back. Over time, this consistency will reinforce the importance of your boundaries to those around you. Surround yourself with people who understand and respect your boundaries. They can offer support and encouragement, making it easier to maintain your stance.

Remind yourself that maintaining boundaries is a healthy and necessary part of self-care. Let go of any guilt or shame associated with keeping certain family members out of your Kitchen. Practice self-compassion. Understand that prioritizing your well-being is not selfish; it's essential. Give yourself permission to do what's best for you.

Sometimes, people push back because they don't understand. Take the time to educate them about the importance of boundaries and how they contribute to healthier relationships. Once someone is in your Kitchen, regardless of who they are, do not give up your boundaries. Ensure you regularly assess your boundaries and the people in your Kitchen. Relationships and circumstances can change, so it's important to ensure that your boundaries still serve your best interests.

Never should you feel guilt or shame for speaking what you want and how others should treat you.

Overview of the Kitchen: Not all family members deserve a place in your Kitchen, and that's okay. It's crucial to prioritize relationships that support and uplift you, maintaining boundaries to protect your well-being. By doing so, you create a safe, nurturing environment for yourself and those who truly belong in your Kitchen. Remember, it's your space, and you have the right to decide who gets to be in it. This is your personal space to fill with people you want in your Kitchen. Remember, no one but you knows who is in which room. You may act the same to them on the outside, but your personal goals, ambitions, and life challenges are for you and your chosen people in your room.

The Inner Circle:
Kitchen Confidants

CHAPTER 6

The Rooms at Work

This subject deserves an entire book, and I am currently gathering additional research. Building friendships at work is different from making friends outside of it; different rules and levels of discretion apply. Workplace friendships can be more complex, shaped by both personal and professional boundaries, which can sometimes blur. Because of these unique dynamics, I've included a section specifically for navigating work-related friendships.

In the workplace, trust is built carefully, but the stakes are different, and betrayals can feel particularly complicated. Work friendships offer support and camaraderie, but they also require a level of awareness and caution that other friendships might not. Understanding these distinctions helps in creating meaningful, supportive relationships at work without crossing boundaries that could impact both your career and personal well-being.

Early in my career, I was unsure of myself and had no idea about office politics. I shared personal and business goals too freely, much like in my personal life. I wanted to be accepted and never took the time to ask myself what I thought of the situation. Looking back, anyone who knew me then would probably say I was lost and unaware of my own identity, and I would have to agree. As a business owner, I have learned, either in office or remote settings, that having these boundaries will help you navigate your career in a positive and productive way. Nothing brings the morale of the company down faster than a betrayal at work.

Over the years, I learned that office team members have boundaries as well. Understanding these boundaries helped me determine who I could share information, ideas, and my next moves at work with. The rooms at the office are the Cubicle, Conference Room, Break Room, and the Car.

The Cubicle

The Cubicle represents the acquaintance, the person you know only at work and do not associate with outside. This might be someone you don't trust or perhaps don't know well enough to establish a deeper bond. You would greet this person in the mornings or participate in office chatter when they are around, but nothing more than pleasant exchanges happen at the Cubicle. This is where everyone starts out, especially in the first few weeks at work, and where you guard all your goals and secrets. In this space, you may pop by to ask for a pen or how to use the copy machine—just the basic necessities to function at work.

Conference Room

The Conference Room is where we are a bit more open, but not much more. We are friends at work and share a few ideas, but we remain guarded with little personal disclosure. You need to work with them more to ensure you can share information safely. At this stage, you might confide in something smaller and see if it spreads through the office. You will chat about kids and maybe express frustrations, but nothing you wouldn't want everyone to hear about.

Here, you discuss work-related topics, share ideas, and collaborate on projects. It's important to maintain a professional demeanor and not overshare personal information. Focus on building a reputation for reliability and competence.

Break Room

The Break Room is where you interact with close friends at work. You share your aspirations but not the specifics of how you will achieve them or your long-term goals. You might hang out with these colleagues outside of work, sharing personal information and seeking their perspective on workplace issues. You discuss how situations make you feel without gossiping about others. (Refer to the chapter on the difference between gossip and sharing for more details.)

This is a space where you can relax a bit and engage in more casual conversations. However, it's still important to be mindful of your boundaries. While you might share a bit more about your personal life here, avoid discussing sensitive topics or office gossip. This is a place to build camaraderie and rapport without compromising your professionalism.

Car

The Car is the place for private conversations with a trusted coworker when you don't want anyone else to hear. The Break Room has too many ears, and the local restaurant might have someone nearby, so the Car becomes the go-to spot for personal discussions. This is someone you have trusted for a while, with whom you have shared little personal information, and who has earned your trust. You treat each other with respect, help with bigger projects, and look out for each other. It's not just about sharing at work; here, you will share your dreams and hopes for work. If they are in your Car, you likely have a personal relationship with them outside of work. If not, but you still feel close, remember that in your real life, they may be on your Porch. You need to experience them outside of work with your family and other friends before they move into your home as well.

The Car represents the closest relationships you have at work—those few colleagues you trust deeply and might even consider friends. These are the people you can confide in about your career aspirations, personal challenges, and more sensitive topics. However, even with these trusted individuals, it's crucial to maintain some level of professional discretion to protect your personal and professional integrity.

When I was going into the office every day at our contracting company, I was the one who picked up on the vibes of the office, what was happening and who was having a bad day. Being in the car is the safest place. I would ask that person, "Hey, I'm going to get office supplies for the team. Why don't you come help me?" This was where they could be vulnerable and really share what was happening.

The Rooms at Work with Clients

This Rooms at Work idea does not end with team members; if you are business to business or even business to consumer, you must be aware of the rooms with your clients. Let's take a look at the following example.

> You have a long-term client whom you trust and value the relationship, they ask you to help them out and make an introduction to another client of yours. This client is in the Break Room with you; you can be honest and have built your business relationship with mutual respect. You are happy to help and offer that introduction.
>
> You have met this person in the past and did not find any red flags that would prevent you from making the introduction. The meeting is set, and you have prepared the individual for who they are about to meet, their motivations, communication style and how to approach them.
>
> You arrive at the meeting and personalities have changed, social cues were off, they did not take into consideration what you shared with them about their communication

preferences. You feel your reputation with the current client is being jeopardized.

The meeting is over, and now you feel damage control needs to take place. You call the client you made the introduction with and explain the situation and that had you known, you would have never set up the meeting, that you appreciate his time. If the relationship is as you believe, it will not jeopardize the long-standing relationship.

However, later, your client's friend would like to know how the meeting went. This is where you need to create business boundaries with the client you made the introduction to—this one is now at the Cubical. Maintain professionalism; however, nothing personal is shared and no inside information about clients or the business. Due to the behavior at the meeting, the client is unpredictable, and you need to protect your reputation as well.

As a professional, maintaining clear boundaries at work is essential, especially when dealing with clients and networking. In this scenario, you have a long-standing, good relationship with a client who asks for a favor—to be introduced to another client of yours. Trusting the mutual respect and honesty that has been the foundation of your business relationship, you agree to facilitate this introduction.

You have previously met the individual who requested the introduction, and having observed no red flags, you feel comfortable proceeding. With due diligence, you prepare them for the meeting, briefing them on the prospective client's motivations, communication style, and the best approach to take.

However, upon attending the meeting, you are met with a surprise. The individual you prepared is not the one who shows up. Instead, it's someone else who clearly does not understand the audience and whose behavior jeopardizes your reputation with your client.

After the meeting, the individual's friend, who is also your client, inquires about how it went. This is a critical moment when establishing and enforcing business boundaries becomes paramount. The individual in question did not listen to your advice, lacked respect during the meeting, and displayed behavior that could potentially disrupt your professional relationships with both clients.

Given this individual's disregard for professional boundaries and emotional control, it's likely they would not take your feedback constructively. They might even react by contacting their friend and the new connections they've made, possibly leading to embarrassing situations and jeopardizing the professional integrity you've worked hard to build.

In such a case, it's important to be tactful in your response. It's clear that this person may not be ready for growth and may not show the necessary restraint, thus crossing professional boundaries. They have demonstrated that they cannot be trusted with personal or sensitive information.

In response to your client's inquiry about the meeting, it would be wise to provide a measured and professional summary without divulging personal opinions or detailed criticism. This approach helps you maintain your professionalism and the trust of your clients while setting clear boundaries regarding what you will and will not tolerate in your business interactions. While they are not in the Cubical, their friend is and will need to maintain the boundary of someone in the Cubical when it comes to their friend.

Without going into great detail, as they have not established that they can be trusted with honest feedback without being reactionary, mention that you have not spoken to the client about the meeting and are unsure how they felt. If they are open to some suggestions, you could offer a couple that might help in future meetings. Once they agree, you might say:

> "In all meetings, it helps to know your audience. As I mentioned before the meeting, they are conservative individuals, and the cursing could have been off-putting for them. For me, first meetings are usually casual; I don't ask for anything and instead look for how I can help them and understand their pain points. Look for clues to see if they want to talk further or change the subject to take the pressure off."

The individual who attended the meeting demonstrated that they are not ready to be in a more trusted position, such as the Conference Room, but rather should be kept at a more guarded level, such as the Cubicle. They have shown they share others' information and took the information you provided as a helpful tool to the meeting without considering how it would reflect on you to the client. This can be seen as giving away information that took you years of respect to learn.

Toxic Positivity in the Workplace

Toxic positivity is the overgeneralization of a happy, optimistic state that results in the denial, minimization, and invalidation of the authentic human emotional experience. This mindset insists that people remain positive and look on the bright side, even in the face of serious challenges or distressing situations. While maintaining a positive outlook can be beneficial, toxic positivity dismisses and disallows the full spectrum of human emotions, which can be harmful in the long run. In other words, you could feel gaslighted by these types of individuals, which can make you rethink your position and end up unable to trust your own judgment. Not to mention, you will feel like you are not being heard.

Signs of Toxic Positivity

- Dismissal of Negative Emotions: Statements like "Just stay positive" or "It could be worse" when someone expresses their struggles.
- Shaming or Guilt: Making someone feel guilty for feeling sad, anxious, or worried.
- Hiding True Feelings: Pretending to be happy all the time and suppressing negative emotions.
- Minimizing Other's Experiences: Downplaying other people's problems or feelings by insisting they "just think positive."
- Overly Optimistic Statements: Pushing unrealistic optimism in all situations, regardless of context.

How to Avoid Toxic Positivity

- Recognize and validate your own and others' feelings, whether they are positive or negative. It's okay to feel sad, angry, or frustrated.

- Create a safe space for people to express their true emotions without fear of judgment or dismissal.
- Instead of offering platitudes, listen actively and show understanding and compassion.
- While it's good to encourage hope and optimism, also acknowledge the reality of the situation and the challenges involved.
- Understand that it's normal to have ups and downs and that not every situation can be spun into a positive light.

By recognizing the signs of toxic positivity and taking steps to foster a more balanced and empathetic approach to emotions, you can create a healthier and more supportive environment for yourself and others.

> BethAnne is a work acquaintance. We would network together, as we had the same target market. Because we were in sales, we had the same mindset and energy level and could bounce ideas off each other. It was nice to have someone like-minded to hang out with, as the company I was working for only had one person in sales and business development—that was me. We became friends and shared ideas and contacts. We would share costs for events and when she needed someone to help sponsor, I

would be there to help. I was strongly under the impression that we were friends, not just work acquaintances. She shared just enough information with me to create a connection, and out of friendship, I was asked to do little favors that would require time and sometimes money. I didn't mind; after all, we were friends, and I thought, "She will do the same for me when I need it."

Everything was going well until I started hearing rumors about what I shared being repeated. I still pushed it aside, thinking, "It's fine. I'm sure it just slipped out." But it wasn't—more and more people were starting to tell me what was being said. Still, I had not changed the way I communicated with her.

One day, I was asked a very big favor, and I was sold on the idea that the exposure would be unlike anything else for the company. She implied that, as a friend, I should do it.

I found out later that I was being manipulated; I was not a true friend and was used to get this favor. You would think I learned my lesson, but I didn't. This relationship would continue for many years, a phone call here and there: "Would you help me with this? You are so good at it. I could really use your expertise. I'm so grateful you are helping me." All the buzzwords someone with few boundaries loves to hear.

I came to realize that when I asked for a favor, she was too busy or promised to help and then did not. She wanted to start a project with me and asked if I could set it up, and we would talk each week about the task for the next week.

Again, hearing, "You are the only one I would do this with. I can work with anyone, but I chose you." I came to realize I would be doing all the work, and she would take the credit. How I didn't realize this earlier was frustrating for me. I was frustrated with myself. I fell victim to this role because I was needed. I was given just enough to take me to the next task and did not see her for who she was.

Once I understood the room she belonged in, I acted accordingly. In this scenario, she was at the Curb. While I no longer shared information, I was able to work with her with stricter boundaries. I no longer provided favors; however, I did meet with her to discuss industry news. She tried a few times after that, her usual "I could really use your expertise; let's exchange talents," but I understood where in the house she belonged, and she did not earn the right to favors. Her words and actions did not match. I was able to keep my boundaries without being disrespectful, rude, or apologetic. I haven't heard from her in years. I was someone she could no longer get anything from without contributing. I was no longer useful to her.

If we connect with like-minded people, then should they understand who we are and not disrespect us? Yes and no—no, not every friend or relationship has the mental capacity to pick up on social cues or respect individual boundaries. Why are boundaries needed with friends or work associates? Some friends lack the self-awareness to create healthy boundaries for themselves; therefore, as in all relationships, we need to show others how we want to be treated.

As in the case of BethAnn, while I have never had this conversation with her, based on how she interacts with others, she does not have enough self-awareness to know or does not care she is using everyone around her as long as she wins. To be honest, when you have boundaries, they can be on whatever journey they are on because you have created your own journey.

In all relationships, we have different levels of being self-aware. We have different ways in which we want to feel valued and understood; therefore, we create boundaries, but what happens when we grow as people? Let's be honest—not everyone has our best interests at heart.

Additional Tips for Navigating Office Politics and Boundaries

Before sharing any personal or sensitive information, assess the level of trust and the nature of your relationship with the colleague. Start with small, non-sensitive topics and gradually share more as trust builds.

Pay attention to how others navigate office politics. Observe who is trusted, who is respected, and how they interact with others. This can provide valuable insights into how to manage your own office relationships.

Be clear about your own boundaries and respect those of others. If someone shares something in confidence, respect their privacy.

Similarly, be clear about what you are comfortable sharing and what you are not.

Always maintain a professional demeanor, especially in shared spaces like the Conference Room and Break Room. Avoid engaging in gossip or negative talk, as this can damage your reputation and relationships.

Regularly reflect on your interactions with colleagues. Consider what went well, what didn't, and how you can improve. This self-awareness can help you build stronger, more effective relationships.

By understanding and respecting these different 'rooms' and the boundaries they represent, you can build healthy, productive relationships at work. This approach will help you stay focused on your goals, maintain your mental strength, and navigate the complex landscape of office politics with confidence and integrity.

Where Do Your Work Friends Belong?

CHAPTER 7

Wrapping It Up

A s you can see, the relational Rooms in Your House are crucial not only for personal relationships but also for business
interactions. Maintaining boundaries is a key component of
preserving your mental health. Throughout our lives, from childhood
to adulthood, we experience changes that necessitate the reevaluation
of our relationships. Maintaining healthy relationships is vital for
personal growth and meaningful human connections.

Understanding that not everyone is ready to be in your Living
Room or Kitchen is also important, as they, too, are managing their
own life's challenges. Go back to Chapter One, where you completed
the assignment to help you determine which room everyone in your
life should occupy.

By now, you should have a list of people in your life, the rooms
they belong in, and the reasons why. Utilize this list to establish new
boundaries. If you had someone in your Kitchen and, after reading the
book, determined they should be on your Porch, then adjust your level
of intimacy and vulnerability to match a Porch-like disclosure. On the

Porch, you will not share deep conversations or overshare personal problems; instead, you will keep conversations to social subjects.

If someone is at a Level Three on your Porch, the conversations can be more personal but still cautious. Do not divulge too much information until they have shown they are trustworthy. For me, Level One involves very superficial information, while at Level Three, I start to share more of my personal goals and frustrations.

What Your List May Look Like:
Example:

- Wally - Kitchen: Husband, known since I was seventeen, has never betrayed my trust.
- Katherine - Curb: Known for two months, not enough history to trust deeply.

The "Rooms in Your House" serves as a tool to help decide where individuals should be placed in your life, ensuring that appropriate information is shared. In other words, we need to protect our boundaries and avoid oversharing. Not everyone has our best interests at heart.

Curb Overview

The Curb is the initial place for new relationships. When you first meet someone, this is where they should start. It's also where some relationships may remain permanently. The Curb acts as a transition zone, allowing time for the relationship to take its natural course. Here, you can observe and evaluate: will they stay at the Curb, or will they move to the Porch? This stage is crucial for determining the potential depth of the relationship without exposing yourself to unnecessary risks.

Porch Overview

The Porch is where most people will stay. For me, I have three levels within this zone, although you may prefer just one step depending on your level of comfort before allowing someone into the Living Room. The Porch is for individuals who are enjoyable to be around, those who share fun stories and vacation experiences, and those who enjoy socializing. However, it is not until Level Three that I share personal information.

This area represents a transitional zone where one decides how much to share with others. Maintaining adequate boundaries here can shield you from being emotionally drained and provide control over the influx of information. For individuals who do not reciprocate or are unable to engage in a deeper relationship, this is where they will remain. By keeping these relationships on the Porch, you can enjoy their company without compromising your emotional well-being.

Living Room Overview

The Living Room is reserved for the people you know well and who have demonstrated they are safe and trustworthy. You can share intimate information, dreams, and hopes for the future with them. These individuals support you and genuinely want to see you succeed. They do not actively try to sabotage your efforts or engage in negative competition. While they may use you as inspiration, it is never at the cost of your well-being.

Having people in this room is essential for human connection. We seek honest feedback and advice from those we trust to tell us the truth. As social creatures, we need these connections for emotional support and growth. The people in the Living Room form your core support system.

Kitchen Overview

The Kitchen is the most trusted room in the house. This space is re-served for a very small circle of individuals you can count on—your "ride or die" companions. While the Living Room and Kitchen may seem inherently safe, it is crucial to maintain boundaries here as well. Although you are less guarded in these spaces, boundaries are still necessary to show others how you want to be treated. Maintaining these boundaries ensures that even your closest relationships remain healthy and respectful.

Learning about the relational Rooms in Your House has enabled me and thousands of people to achieve personal growth. By being careful with our boundaries and sharing only with those who have our best interests at heart, we can let go of shame and step into a journey of self-love and acceptance. This journey allows you to reclaim your power and learn to trust your own judgment again, ultimately becoming the person you've always known you are.

We have learned the difference between gossip and sharing and how this distinction can affect relationships. By reducing negativity and establishing a more positive circle around you, you create an environment conducive to growth and well-being.

By creating boundaries, we enable constructive communication that benefits both parties in the relationship. This allows us to reflect on challenges and move toward healthy solutions. Understanding the Rooms in Your House helps us explore the importance of nurturing relationships, both personal and professional, and how they can be cultivated. We invest energy into relationships that are worthy of being in the Living Room, which leads to enjoying the people around us more and no longer having unrealistic expectations.

In summary, the concept of Rooms in Your House serves as a powerful tool for managing relationships and maintaining mental and emotional health. It helps you identify who belongs in each space, ensuring that your interactions are meaningful and supportive. This approach promotes a balanced life filled with strong, healthy relationships. While this is a lifelong learning and self-improvement process, it eventually becomes second nature. The more we utilize these new skills, the less we attract negative and unhealthy people into our lives, and we no longer draw the wrong types of individuals toward us.

We understand the importance of setting realistic and meaningful goals for each room with the people we meet. We are in control of what we share and how much others can share with us. This allows us to enjoy individuals for who they are, not for what we think they should be.

I hope that you embrace the concept of the Rooms in Your House, name them what you want, and learn to appreciate all kinds of people in your life, whether they are there for a season or a reason. By knowing which room they belong to, you can take in what they offer as a gift of learning and appreciation. This can only enhance your life.

If you have not done so already, I suggest you take some time to evaluate each person in your life and determine which room they belong in based on their actions and past history. Keep this list private, as it is for your eyes only. Revisit this list every month to see if individuals in your life have earned a new room in your house. Have they shown signs of betrayal or demonstrated that they are not someone you prefer to be associated with? Maybe they are not your people. This process may surprise you as you begin to trust your own judgments, providing you with a new sense of who you are and what your values are.

Journal about the people in your life—what you like about them, how they have enriched your life, and how you feel when you are around them. This reflective practice can deepen your understanding of your relationships and help you make more informed decisions about who belongs in each room.

I hope you have found the information in this book helpful as a way to renew your sense of self and encourage you to take your happiness into your own hands. I want you to feel empowered and ready to build healthy friendships that will help you be the best version of yourself.

You can find me on all social media outlets under wendyknipp. Reach out, say hello, and let me know how this has helped you.

Home Inventory: Where Do Your Friends Really Belong?

_____

_____

_____

_____

_____

_____

_____

_____

_____

_____

_____

_____

_____

_____

_____

_____

_____

_____

_____

Acknowledgments

This book is the result of a deeply personal journey—one that I hope will help others learn from my struggles and triumphs in building meaningful friendships. For so long, I sought out connections that often left me feeling empty, but through these pages, I've come to embrace the value of true, unconditional love—the kind of love I am blessed to have in my life.

First and foremost, I want to acknowledge that without my Lord and Savior, Jesus Christ, as my guide in life, I would not be here. The words and ideas in this book come from Him, and all the glory belongs to Him. He has given me the strength and wisdom to navigate the path of healing, and it is by His hand that I have been led to this moment.

To my husband, Wally—my rock, my safe place. You've always given me the courage to be unapologetically myself. You stood by me, unwavering, even when I was uncertain of my path. Through your love, I've learned to trust my feelings and instincts, even when others don't understand. You are my truest friend, and the strength of our bond is the foundation of this entire journey. You are my constant source of support, and for that, I will always be grateful.

To my son, Aaron, my anchor in this world. You've shown me the importance of accountability—both to myself and to others. Your unwavering belief in me has helped me navigate the darkest moments, reminding me never to give up on myself. You've held me to the highest standards, and that's what's made me stronger. You are more than my son—you are my confidant and my eternal ride-or-die.

To my daughter, Ashley, my best friend, my light and my mirror. Your encouragement to push me beyond my comfort zone and pursue relationships that align with my values has been transformative. You've shown me that I deserve friendships that nurture and uplift me. God truly blessed me with you, and I thank Him every day for giving me not only a daughter but also a best friend. You reflect the best parts of me, and through you, I've learned what it means to have someone in my corner who truly understands me.

Wally, Aaron, and Ashley, you are the heart of my life—the people I trust most in my kitchen, the sacred space where only those closest to me belong. When all else fails, I know you have my back, and that kind of love is priceless. You are my legacy, and together we've broken the cycle of dysfunction, building something real, unshakable, and rooted in love. I am honored to be your wife and mom, and to have you by my side.

I would like to extend my deepest gratitude to Steve Rigby, author of *S.M.I.L.E.* and a person of true integrity and commitment. Despite his demanding schedule, he generously took the time to read my manuscript and craft a foreword that truly elevates this work. His authority is evident not only in his words but in the way he leads his life—a living example of the principles he shares. I am honored by his support and inspired by his dedication, and I am incredibly grateful for his valuable contribution to this book.

My heartfelt thanks to Sharon for writing a foreword for this book. Your words carry the strength and wisdom you've shared with me over the years. As a long-time friend and mentor, your leadership and belief in me have not only shaped my journey but profoundly impacted my life. I am honored and deeply grateful to have your voice opening these pages.

A heartfelt thank you to those who took the time not only to read my manuscript but to review it with genuine care, offering thoughtful and invaluable feedback. To Rick, who listened to my stories with patience and shared insightful guidance; to Lisa, who helped me see new perspectives; and to Gala, whose words encouraged me to dig deeper. Each of you read with such dedication, sharing honest reflections. I am deeply grateful for your time, your wisdom, and, above all, your support.

To Beth, who understood my vision from the moment I started talking about the "rooms in your house." You made me feel heard and validated in ways I never had before. You took my words and helped organize my thoughts, knowing that this book came from a place of love. Thank you for grasping the heart of my message and helping me to shape something that would not shame others, but instead release the shame so many of us carry from dysfunctional friendships. Your insight and compassion were invaluable.

I'm deeply grateful to my friend and counselor, Cinthia—you have helped me find the words to articulate my feelings, you guided me through my emotions and helped me make sense of them. You gave me the tools to grow and thrive.

And to my father's family, especially Bob and Grace and my father's siblings, whose house stands as a symbol of our shared history and legacy, thank you for the foundation you built, both in bricks and in spirit.

After developing the "rooms in your house," I was able to form incredible friendships in my personal and work life and find true friends who love and want the best for me. While I wish I could name them all, I risk hurting those I don't mention, but please know that each of you has made a lasting impact on my life.

This book is for anyone who has ever felt lost in their friendships or has longed for genuine connection. It's a reminder that true friendships aren't about quantity, but about quality—those who love you unconditionally and stand by your side through it all.

Thank you to everyone who has been part of this journey. Your love and support made this book possible.

About the Author

Wendy Knipp is a relationship expert, speaker, and author with a passion for helping people navigate the complex world of friendships and personal boundaries. With over ten years of experience in life coaching and personal development, Wendy has dedicated her career to empowering individuals to create healthier relationships with themselves and more fulfilling relationships with others.

Drawing on a wealth of professional expertise and personal experiences, Wendy has developed a unique approach to understanding and managing friendships, which is beautifully encapsulated in her latest book, *The Rooms in Your House*. Known for her engaging storytelling and practical advice, Wendy has a talent for breaking down complex emotional concepts into relatable and actionable insights.

A sought-after speaker at numerous conferences and workshops, Wendy's compassionate and down-to-earth style resonates with audiences of all ages, making her teachings accessible and impactful.

When not writing or speaking, Wendy enjoys traveling, playing tennis, reading, and spending time with her husband of thirty-four years and their two children. She and her husband were married in 1990 and have been together since 1984. Wendy is an avid believer in the power of authentic connections. She lives in Arizona, where she continues to inspire and guide others on their journey toward stronger, healthier relationships.

To connect with Wendy, visit www.wendyknipp.com.

Made in the USA
Monee, IL
07 January 2025

39d7d465-ef2e-46b2-8af3-2813e3b7f5d7R01